THE OUTTRAVELER

NEW YORK CITY

DAN ALLEN

alyson books
NEW YORK

THIS TRADE PAPERBACK ORIGINAL IS PUBLISHED BY

Alyson Books
245 West 17th Street
New York, NY 10011

DISTRIBUTION IN THE UNITED KINGDOM BY

Turnaround Publisher Services Ltd.
Unit 3, Olympia Trading Estate
Coburg Road, Wood Green
London N22 6TZ England

FIRST EDITION: *April 2008*

08   09   10   11   12   a   10   9   8   7   6   5   4   3   2   1

ISBN-10 1-59350-066-1
ISBN-13 978-1-59350-066-5

Library of Congress Cataloging–in–Publication data are on file.

Design by **VICTOR MINGOVITS**
Photography by **GÁBOR LADISZLAI**

As the editor in chief of The Out Traveler, *I'm delighted at the launch of our new travel series.* The Out Traveler *strives to inspire sophisticated readers like you by showcasing thoughtful and transformative travel experiences that set the standard of gay travel. These books, which emphasize the long-overlooked, but incredibly powerful cultural and historical traditions of our community throughout the world, help us reach this goal.*

—ED SALVATO
EDITOR IN CHIEF, *The Out Traveler*
CORPORATE DIRECTOR OF TRAVEL MEDIA
AT PLANETOUT INC.

ABOUT THE AUTHOR

DAN ALLEN is a New York City-based writer and longtime contributor to virtually every major national gay publication including *The Out Traveler, The Advocate, Out, Instinct,* and *Passport,* as well as such mainstream outlets as the *Miami Herald.* Born and raised in Grand Rapids, Michigan, Allen majored in filmand television at NYU's Tisch School of the Arts before moving to Los Angeles to pursue Hollywood screenwriting fame. Instead, he served stints as

Rob Lowe's personal assistant and editor of the biweekly Southern California gay entertainment guide *Planet Homo*. A seasoned travel copywriter, Allen has also written extensively for the tourism boards of Thailand, Spain, and France. Two years ago he gleefully returned to New York, where his current East Village home is just a few blocks from the street corner scene of his first NYC job some 25 years ago—passing out flyers for the Pyramid Club.

THE OUT TRAVELER PHILOSOPHY

Yes, we know: On your travels around the globe (or even close to home), you've plowed through your fair share of dry, Yellow Page-like guidebooks aimed at the most massive of mass markets. Sure, they may include a tiny gay section that makes a token nod to you, but little else. Moreover, many guides seem to rely so heavily on throwing as much soon-to-be-outdated information at you, that you are left wondering about the deeper aspects of a place. How is it unique from others? What's it like to live there? How is being gay there different from other places? What are the more meaningful things I need to know to really understand where I'm going?

Our vision with this guidebook is born from the same desire we share with *The Out Traveler* magazine. We aim to give you the expert tools that will not only lend practicality to your journey, but also cultural and historical insight, understanding, and intimate appreciation of where you're going—and of course, how to do it all in style.

THE LGBT TRAVELER

Loosened from the bonds of tradition and societal expectations, gay and lesbian people have been trailblazers throughout human history. And it's no different with our distinctive take on travel. Queer people have frequently had to sojourn to distant shores to find our true "homes." We often understand a place and discover its layers years before our heterosexual comrades do. As the globe opens up even further in the 21st century to welcome us, offering more places than ever for the LGBT traveler to visit, we still need to explore the world with our eyes wide open. Perhaps it's part of our special survival skill set: Queer people have to know where we are welcome, how to fit in, the vibe of a particular cultural or political climate—all things many straights take for granted. In a word, we are savvy. And innovative. And our authors strive to reflect that innate intelligence in our guidebooks. We want to impart to you the travel tools for deeper understanding. After all, even the slightest of vacations is meant to be transformative.

THE OUT TRAVELER GUIDES

Instead of throwing in the (shallow) kitchen sink, we present you with our knowledgeable, hand-picked recommendations. We cull, interview, visit, and delve deeply to find both the gay and mainstream establishments we feel fit well with sophisticated queer sensibility, with an emphasis on the luxurious, the classy, or at least the truly unique. You'll also find reference to our Web site, OUTTRAVELER. COM, where loads more up-to-the-minute articles, listings, and information on a particular locale can be found. In our *Out Traveler* guidebooks, we spend time exploring the distinct history, politics, and the unexpected quirks of a place in order for you to become a sharp traveler, not just a fly-by-night tourist. If we can illuminate a locale's soul for you, then we have done our job.

No establishment has paid to be in our guides—you are getting our often opinionated take on what we feel is worthwhile. Our authors are personally involved in the places they write about, often having resided in the destination for years. Nothing beats local, on-the-ground insider expertise. Our authors give you pertinent knowledge on local laws and attitudes toward gays in our signature *Out Traveler* ratings boxes found in every chapter.

So sit back and let us take you on a trip. Travel is profoundly personal and frequently life changing. Let us help you discover the essence of what the journey is all about.

CONTENTS

CHAPTER 4

LOWER MANHATTAN, CHINATOWN,
AND TRIBECA 67

CHAPTER 9

UPPER EAST SIDE, UPPER WEST SIDE, HARLEM AND WASHINGTON HEIGHTS

CHAPTER 10

BROOKLYN, QUEENS, BRONX, AND STATEN ISLAND

Web links on **OutTraveler.com**

NEW YORK CITY WEB LINKS AND
TIPS ON OUTTRAVELER.COM

NEW YORK CITY AND ME

My first trip to New York City was as an excitable eight-year-old on the only road trip my parents and I ever took beyond the Midwest, in what could best be described as *The Out-of-Towners, with Child* (if you've never seen the 1970 Jack Lemon/Sandy Dennis film classic, you should, but bear in mind that the city's not quite the same unforgiving place to yokels it was then). I can still vividly remember our arrival at the Holiday Inn on 57th Street, where we were met by a loud bellman who to my dad's dismay insisted on escorting us and our bags up to our room, all the while repeatedly reciting in thick New York-ese the story of his last encounter with a family of vacationing Midwesterners, who after all his tireless luggage-toting toil "only gave me a quodda." As the pushy porter informed us several times, he'd refused the coin, proudly telling the skinflint father, "Keep it. Go buy your kid an ice cream cone." My dad, a skinflint himself but no match for such aggressive New York passive/aggressiveness, came through with a whole dollar.

While I delighted in wonders like the Statue of Liberty and the Empire State Building over the next few days, I could pretty easily sense that my normally mellow parents were operating in a state of constant nervous hysteria amidst the hustle and bustle of a city that wasn't showing them a lot of mercy. On the morning we left town, Dad was so anxious to get out that he hastily parked our car in front of the hotel while retrieving Mom and me, only to find upon our return that it'd been towed. This induced another of my most distinct early New York memories; that of my mother sobbing quietly in the back of a cab en route to the tow yard. Hundreds of 1970s dollars later, we were safely back in our car, and the joy of imminent escape was palpable.

But the city still had one more surprise up its sleeve on this late June 1972 Sunday afternoon. Dad wanted to swing downtown to glimpse the almost complete World Trade Center, but hadn't counted on a traffic-stopping protest march. As we watched from the sidelines, a procession of odd-looking characters streamed past, the likes of which I'd never seen before. "Daddy, what are they doing?" I asked. "Oh, they're just a bunch of clowns," said Pops. They didn't look like any kind of clowns I knew. Crazy hair and big smiles maybe, but where were the rubber noses and oversized shoes? Only much later did I realize that we'd borne firsthand witness to the third New York City Gay Liberation Day March.

I didn't return to the city until I was an adult, if only barely. As part of a fairly tumultuous period coming both of age and out, several fellow art-homo Michiganders and I decided to spend spring break 1983 in Manhattan, where we shacked up at the Hotel Chelsea. Almost instantly we were swept up into the then–überhot Danceteria club scene, so irreparably that our week-long visit morphed into a month, and then six. By day we lived in squalor, crashing on fluid-stained mattresses, four to a room (plus the roaches) that was barely big enough for one. But it was enough for us to be cool by night, hanging out in the midst of Klaus Nomi,

Andy Warhol, John Sex, Madonna, and a host of the day's other biggest downtown luminaries. Fortunately for my health my money ran out, and I skulked back to the Midwest.

After detox, life reassessment, and two years of film school in Chicago, I transferred back to NYU to finish up my BFA at Tisch. My New York experience this go-round was far less glamorous, but certainly no less colorful. I lived on Mulberry Street in what was then still Little Italy, sharing a first floor railroad-style apartment that had last been occupied by the mother of a mob boss. Italian ladies dotted the windowsills above our block, keeping a constant watchful eye on everything that transpired below. Our building's prime matriarch was Dolly, who started my every morning with a hearty, "Hi Danny, howwayuh?" The loud cracks of Fed line-tapping syncopated every phone conversation, and every Wednesday night the street would fill with black Mercedeses from John Gotti's

GENETIC DÉJÀ VU

I didn't know it until researching this book, but my DNA seems to have actually made it to New York City a long time before I ever did. Not only was one of my ninth great-grandfathers (a Walloon immigrant named Pierre Billiou) one of the first settlers of Staten Island (his 1664 house, still standing, is the oldest structure there), but another ninth great-grandfather (Coenradt Ten Eyck) came to New Amsterdam in 1651 and owned the land at the southern tip of Manhattan that would give the name to the present-day Coenties Slip. Sadly, our branch of the family seems not to have inherited any claim to either property.

weekly wiseguy summit, held literally opposite our place. We were burgled once, and our heretofore unseen (and never seen again) landlord appeared at our door as if from central casting. When he told me who he was, I went to shake his hand, only to realize it was missing a few fingers. "If I ever find out who did this," he assured me ominously, "they'll pay." Never have I believed anyone so fully.

After graduation I opted to switch coasts to Los Angeles to pursue a screenwriting career, but as fate would have it instead I worked a string of entertainment industry jobs before morphing back into writing. In the interim I made several memorable visits back to New York. In 1990 I spent a week here with my then-boss Rob Lowe when he hosted *Saturday Night Live.* In '94 I came for the twenty-fifth anniversary of the Stonewall riots, and I was here six years later when Hillary Clinton took part in her first NYC Pride Parade. And I came for the final Wigstock on Chelsea Pier over Labor Day weekend in 2001, just days before 9/11. Not long after that I started caring for my wonderful mom, who'd contracted Alzheimer's. When she passed rather poetically on the last day of 2005, I knew it was time to finally leave L.A. behind and come home to New York for good.

I've been back for two years now, and I've loved every minute of it. I love the sights, I love the smells, I love the convergence of cultures, I love the random bits of overheard conversation, and I love that I never know what I'm going to experience the next time I walk out my front door. I live in the East Village, just a few blocks away from the scene of my first-ever job in the city, handing out flyers for the Pyramid Club, unbelievably 25 years ago now. The neighborhood's changed a lot since then, as has the whole town, and I can't say that I'm crazy about all of the changes. The Hotel Chelsea is currently being "cleaned up" and transformed into a boutique property, and the first floor Mulberry Street apartment from my NYU days is now a trendy Nolita dress shop. On the other hand, the Pyramid was recently nominated by the Greenwich Village Society of Historic Preservation as the city's first potential drag landmark. But they're all just buildings anyway. And at the end of the day, New York's soul has very little to do with its bricks and steel, and everything to do with its people, of which I feel lucky every day to be one.

—DAN ALLEN

NEW YORK CITY LGBT HISTORY:
HOW WE GOT SO HERE, SO QUEER, AND SO USED TO IT

For gay people around the world, New York City is inexorably tied to our collective history; the events at the Stonewall Inn that fateful late June 1969 evening certainly not marking the first time a gay bar was ever raided, nor even the first time people got mad and rose up in dissent. But something changed on that hot Village evening, a paradigm shift that would galvanize us forever going forward into standing up for our right to be who we are, and to not feel ashamed nor let ourselves be pushed around any longer. It's a place and time now etched on the collective global gay consciousness, so much so that in Germany and Switzerland, Gay Pride is still called CSD (Christopher Street Day) in honor of the first anniversary liberation celebration held in New York in 1970.

But Stonewall's fame is also a burden for gay history, for so strong is its symbol that many in today's LGBT generation actually presume that we had no culture prior to 1969; that maybe there were gay people, but they were trapped in dark closets of self-loathing. Nothing, my brothers and sisters, could be further from the truth.

Gay people have been settling in New York City since people in general have been settling here. We know this not because they left behind flyers for some hot colonial man club, but because records reveal that two of the first three executions in New Amsterdam, in 1646 and 1660, were for sodomy. The first, a black slave, was publicly choked to death and then burned. The second, a Dutch soldier, was tied in a sack and thrown into what is now New York Harbor. Not a very auspicious start for the city's gay scene.

Our fate changed dramatically when the English took power, even going so far as to install a transvestite (Edward Hyde, Lord Cornbury) as governor of New York and New Jersey from 1701 to 1708. We don't know if Hyde was gay (he was married, and seems to have enjoyed fondling his wife's ears), and we don't even know for sure that the cross-dressing claim wasn't just invented by his political enemies. But there is a painting of one very unattractive lady at the New York Historical Society that's got his name on it. And we know that he's actor Cary Elwes's direct ancestor, but that's neither here nor there.

The next century or so is a bit of a Dark Ages for gay New York City history, but we can assume that we were around and that we were finding places to rendezvous Revolution-style. As the 1800s progressed, certain areas of the city (like around City Hall) became known gay cruising areas, and by 1846 there was at least one male brothel on the Bowery. Already a young Walt Whitman was walking the city's streets, and through his poetry he would soon share with the world one passionate New York gay man's take on life.

Various gay nightspots cropped up in the ensuing decades, probably most notoriously The Slide on Bleecker Street, which in 1890 the *New York Press* called "the wickedest place on earth," where the patrons were "effeminate, degraded and addicted to vices which are inhuman and unnatural." Though The Slide was shut down in 1892, three years later there were still half a dozen "resorts" in the city (most on Bowery or close to it) catering to fairies and their friends. While some apparently offered raucous entertainment, prostitution was clearly a heavy component and probably the main attraction for men who came from better parts of the city to "slum it."

By the early years of the 20th century, gays wanting something a little more than trade had developed codes as a way to spot one another on New York City streets, the apparent favorites being green suits and red ties (though not together, unless it was Christmas). For those who found such garments gaudy, bathhouses required no clothing at all. As the gay baths culture took off in the early 1900s, cops seem to have gone back and forth from completely ignoring the establishments to cracking down heavily. In what's thought to be the first raid on a gay bathhouse anywhere, in 1903 they raided the Ariston Baths on 55th Street. Twenty-six men were arrested, and seven were slapped with prison time of up to 20 years.

The 1920s roared wildly in New York City, and in an era when norms were flung by the wayside, gay culture flourished. Bohemian Greenwich Village was becoming one of the biggest hotbeds for this new above-ground gay presence, and by the end of the decade gays and bisexuals like Countee Cullen, Bessie Smith, and Langston Hughes were igniting Harlem's Renaissance Uptown as well. The neighborhood's fantastic drag balls grew larger every year, by the early 1930s drawing thousands including the city's elite. Meanwhile a Pansy Craze developed in Times Square, with Brooklynite Jean Malin leading the charge of a musical movement that would soon sweep the nation.

By the mid-1930s the repeal of Prohibition and the worsening Depression brought an end to the party and a swing in the social more pendulum. Those gay-friendly establishments that managed to weather the downturn faced closure during Mayor LaGuardia's "cleanup" of the city in advance of the 1939 World's Fair. New York City's gay culture was ostensibly forced underground again throughout the 1940s and early '50s, but a new generation managed

THE GREY LADY WEIGHS IN

The paper of record for both the city and the world, the *New York Times* has both covered and reflected the changing climate of society's attitudes toward gay people, as these snippets from just the last half century of its gay culture coverage reveal.

1959 In an article on racial tension in Greenwich Village, the *Times* reports, "Another cause of friction in the neighborhood is the homosexual," since though they mostly segregate in their own bars and on their own street corners, "sometimes...they put on a more flamboyant show of their homosexuality."

1961 *New York Times* critic Howard Taubman attacks what he calls "the increasing incidence of homosexuality on the New York stage."

1963 The *NY Times* publishes a front page article called "Growth of Overt Homosexuality in City Provokes Wide Concern," dubbing "the presence of what is probably the greatest homosexual population in the world and its increasing openness" the city's "most sensitive open secret."

1971 The *NY Times Magazine* prints the first-person "What It Means to Be Homosexual," for the first time putting a face to gay people for a wide mainstream audience.

THE GREY LADY WEIGHS IN

1974 The *NY Times* prints a surprising six-part series entitled "Homosexuals in New York: The Gay World."

1977 "The city's homosexual population, which only a few years ago began to 'come out of the closet and into the streets,' has developed markedly in recent months into a cohesive, open and organized force," says the *Times* in an article called "Homosexuals in New York Find New Pride."

1981 The *NY Times* reports on a "rare cancer seen in 41 homosexuals," mostly in the San Francisco Bay area and New York City.

1982 Of the 335 men with the "new homosexual disorder" reported by the *NY Times*, 158 live in New York City.

1987 The *NY Times* agrees to change its editorial policy and use the word "gay" rather than "homosexual" for the first time.

2002 The Sunday Style section of the *NY Times* publishes same-sex unions alongside heterosexual ones for the first time, and changes the heading from "Weddings" to "Weddings/Celebrations."

to survive and even thrive under the radar. Certain of the city's hotel bars (especially and most famously that at the Astor in Times Square) became known before and after World War II—throughout the city and the wider gay world—as places where gay men could find one another.

Despite (or in response to) the growing conservatism in the rest of the country, the 1950s saw New York emerge as the world's cultural capital, with an exciting onslaught of quasi-openly gay people igniting the city's various arts scenes, from Tennessee Williams to James Baldwin to Truman Capote to Merce Cunningham to Andy Warhol. Greenwich Village resurged as the city's main gay enclave, with Midtown's Third Avenue area (known as "The Bird Circuit") also popular.

As the 1960s dawned, gays had already turned 42nd Street between Seventh and Eighth Avenues into a popular sleazy cruising spot. But the important cultural stuff was happening down in the Village, where closets were opening, prompting the *New York Times* to print a front page article in 1963 entitled "Growth of Overt Homosexuality in City Provokes Wide Concern" (see sidebar). In ominous tones, the piece points out that "identifiable homosexuals—perhaps only half of the total—seem to throng Manhattan's Greenwich Village, the East Side from the upper 40's through the 70's and the West 70's." In 1967 Craig Rodwell opened the Village's Oscar Wilde Bookshop, the first nonporn gay-themed bookstore in the world. In 1968 the city's first Gay Scene Guide appeared, listing more than 100 bars and cruising areas in the NYC area.

Of course 1969 became the flashpoint for the gay rights movement with the police raid of the Stonewall Inn. While some of the folklore surrounding that night (such as that our last gay nerve was already raw from Judy Garland's death less than a week earlier) has been discounted, what's clear is that we weren't going to take the abuse any more. The first Gay Pride march ensued within days, and the Gay Liberation Front formed soon after. A lesser known but perhaps nearly as movement-important raid came less than nine months after Stonewall, when the gay after-hours bar the Snake Pit was invaded in March 1970, after which anyone left doubting there was need for change became thoroughly convinced.

Thanks to the hard, brave work of those post-Stonewall fighters, things did change in the '70s. Closets were flung open citywide, and Greenwich Village became the world's first proud gay ghetto. The tension of pent-up centuries would be unleashed in a decade of sheer gay hedonism, with New York City at its axis. In the early '80s came the first signs of the wake-up call that would become known as AIDS, with New York serving as one of its biggest centers of devastation. The city's gay population suffered extreme losses.

Today, as has long been the case, there is no one gay community in New York City, but rather literally scores of different gay subsets affiliated by location, mindset, body type, or some combination thereof. While Chelsea took over in the 1990s as the city's most identifiable gay ghetto, Greenwich Village is still plenty gay, as are the East Village and strong up-comer Hell's Kitchen. Smaller gay pockets (some homegrown, some formed by new gay settlement) are scattered all over the five boroughs, from Harlem to South Bronx to Jackson Heights to Park Slope to Stapleton. But really, we are everywhere in New York City. Indeed, the city now hosts no fewer than seven separate Gay Prides.

What does the future hold for gay New York City? Possibly Gracie Mansion (the mayor's residence), as current speaker of the New York City Council and open lesbian Christine Quinn is widely expected to run for the city's top spot in 2009.

It's a far cry from the days of being tossed into New York Harbor.

WHEN TO COME

New York is a popular destination year-round, but especially so in summer, and for gay visitors even more especially in June around the various Pride events (see NYC LGBT Events). Spring and fall are actually some of the most pleasant times to visit, with temperatures neither too hot nor too cold, and the either budding or falling leaves putting on a nice sideshow.

WHAT TO PACK

Your clothing needs will depend greatly on the season, but you'll definitely want to bring the best of what you've got in any weather, as New Yorkers dress to impress. In winter be sure to bring a coat, hat, scarf, and gloves (as wind chills can sometimes dip below 0° Fahrenheit), and thick boots if the forecast calls for snow (if you have them, long underwear aren't a bad idea either). In summer you'll want shorts and short-sleeved shirts (as the heat index can often top 100° Fahrenheit), plus the all-important sunglasses and sun block. Comfortable shoes are a must in all weather, as you'll be walking a lot. A portable umbrella could come in handy, though you can always pick one up for cheap here should you need it. If you'll be eating in the city's nicest restaurants, you should bring at least a sport coat. And if possible, leave room in your suitcase for the new stuff you know you'll be going home with. On that note, bring money, and lots of it. No need to bring hard cash as ATMs are everywhere and most places take credit, but be prepared to spend more than you think you will.

GETTING HERE

AIR New York City is served by three main airports: John F. Kennedy (JFK) and LaGuardia (LGA), both in Queens, and Newark (EWR) in New Jersey. Generally speaking, LaGuardia serves domestic U.S. routes while JFK caters to international travel (and some domestic), while Newark does about just as much of each. Which airport you use will likely be dictated by which airline you fly, but if you have a choice, each comes with advantages for the Manhattan-bound traveler. LaGuardia is physically the closest and therefore the quickest and cheapest cab ride into the city, while JFK and Newark both offer fairly simple (but undeniably more stressful) money-saving public transport options. For more information about all three airports (including AirTrain info for Newark and JFK), check the Port Authority of New York & New Jersey Web site (PANYNJ.COM).

FROM THE AIRPORT The chart to the right is a basic overview of about how much each airport transfer option will cost you in money and time. Shuttle prices are from SuperShuttle (SUPERSHUTTLE.COM), car service prices are from Carmel Limousine (800-9CARMEL or 212-666-6666, CARMELLIMO.COM, 800-258-3826), and, for the glamorous, helicopter prices (which are actually quite reasonable) are from US Helicopter (877-262-7676, FLYUSHELICOPTER.COM).

FROM THE AIRPORT TO MANHATTAN

	JFK	LaGUARDIA	NEWARK
HELICOPTER (specified stops)	$140 10 minutes	N/A	$140 10 minutes
CAR SERVICE (add tolls/tip)	$40–$45 35-75 minutes	$28–$35 25-60 minutes	$43–$50 35-75 minutes
TAXI (add tolls/tip)	$45 flat rate 35-75 minutes	$20–$40 25-60 minutes	$30–$50 35-75 minutes
SHARED VAN (add tip)	$21–$23 60-120 minutes	$16 45-90 minutes	$21 60-120 minutes
AIRTRAIN (specified stops)	$7–$12 35-75 minutes	N/A	$15 45-75 minutes

2

CRITICAL NEW YORK CITY INFO FOR THE OUT TRAVELER

RAIL Amtrak (AMTRAK.COM) links virtually every eastern seaboard city with New York; fares are often not much (and sometimes not at all) lower than air rates, but considering the savings on airport transfer it's sometimes worth it. Amtrak, the Long Island Railroad (LIRR), and New Jersey Transit all use Penn Station (31st to 33rd Sts., between Seventh and Eighth Aves.), while Metro-North trains arriving from upstate and Connecticut use Grand Central (42nd to 44th Sts., between Madison and Lexington Aves.).

CAR There are countless ways to arrive into the city by car; none of them are recommended. Delays getting in and out can be long, and parking once you arrive can be either very difficult or very expensive, or both.

BUS Usually far from glamorous, buses are a less than ideal way to get to the city, but they're sometimes the only available option. The vast majority of NYC bus routes use Port Authority Bus Terminal (625 Eighth Ave., between 40th and 42nd Sts.).

GETTING AROUND

PUBLIC TRANSPORT For all of its notoriety as a sort of underground human zoo, New York's subway system is actually quite efficient (all things considered), and one of the few in the world to run 24 hours (though service can be spotty late nights, and on weekends for that matter). With well over 400 stations, the subway's various lines connect all reaches of every borough except Staten Island, which has its own railway. The city also operates an extensive bus line, but since it doesn't have the subway's advantage of bypassing busy streets, it's far less used by locals and certainly tourists.

Fare for both subways and buses is $2 per ride, payable with a MetroCard that can be purchased with cash, debit, or credit card from machines in most stations; a one-day pass is $7.50, weekly $25, 14-day $47, and monthly MetroCard $81. For more info including maps, a trip planner, and service updates, go to the Metropolitan Transit Authority Web site (MTA.INFO/NYCT or MTA.INFO/METROCARD/TOURISM/INDEX.HTML). Free subway maps are also available at the booths in most stations.

TAXI Riding in a New York City taxi has never been easier, since the entire fleet (much to many drivers' consternation) has recently been outfitted with credit card readers—not to mention snazzy new backseat video screens that blast news, ads, and your GPS position at you whether you like it or not. Hailing a cab in the street is simple: Just look for one with a lit middle (medallion number) light on top of the car; if there's no light, the cab already has a passenger; if the OFF DUTY lights are lit on either side of the medallion number light, the cab is not in service. The base fare is $2.50, plus $.40 for each additional unit (1/5 mile or 1 minute of non-motion). There's a peak weekday surcharge of $1 Monday to Friday between 4 and 8 PM, and a $.50 night surcharge between 8 PM and 6 AM. Tipping is generally 10–20%, and usually just rounded up to the appropriate even dollar amount (for example, a $7.10 fare would become $8 even with a $.90 tip). For more info, go to NYC.GOV/TAXI.

CAR RENTAL Unless you've got a very unusual and compelling reason, renting a car in New York is really not a bright idea. Street parking is scarce with confusing rules, and parking lots are ridiculously expensive. Between cabs, the subway, and walking (remember that?), there's absolutely no need for a car in the city.

FACTS AND FIGURES

NYC POPULATION (2006): 8,214,426 *Largest city in the U.S.; 13th largest in the world*

MANHATTAN: 1,611,581

BROOKLYN: 2,508,820

QUEENS: 2,255,175

BRONX: 1,361,473

STATEN ISLAND: 477,377

AVERAGE JANUARY TEMPERATURES: High 38, low 26

AVERAGE JULY TEMPERATURES: High 84, low 69

VISITORS TO NYC (2006): 43.8 million

    DOMESTIC: 36.5 million

    INTERNATIONAL: 7.3 million

HOTEL ROOMS (2007): 72,250

AVERAGE NIGHTLY HOTEL RATE (2007): $295

EATING ESTABLISHMENTS: 18,696

AVERAGE DINNER COST (TAX & TIP INCLUDED, ZAGAT 2006): $39.43

HOTELS

With over 72,000 hotel rooms in New York City, your lodging choices are plentiful—but not cheap. With the average room price hovering around the $300 mark, the cost of your stay can add up very quickly. Unfortunately there aren't many good ways around this inevitability; for most, staying outside of Manhattan doesn't make sense, as the time and money you'll spend getting back and forth will wind up canceling out any hotel savings. There are a few very decent lower cost options around town (we've tried to include as many as possible), but they're mostly small and fill up very quickly, so do plan ahead.

RESTAURANTS

Many of the finer restaurants listed here are world-renowned and exceedingly popular, to the point that getting reservations is something you should think about far in advance (months even) of your visit. OPENTABLE.COM is an excellent resource for checking availability online for most of the city's top eateries. Also be aware that while casual attire is fine at the great majority of NYC's restaurants, many in the top tier require at least a jacket.

A WORD ON PRICES

Since lodging and dining prices tend to change often (and in the case of lodging can vary greatly at the same property depending on how you book), we've chosen to simply put each listing in a basic cost category: **INEXPENSIVE** (lodging below $200 per night, dining below about $15 per entrée), **MODERATE** (lodging $200–$400, dining $15–$30), **EXPENSIVE** (lodging $400–$600, dining $30–$60), and in a few cases **VERY EXPENSIVE** (lodging over $600, dining over $60).

NYC LGBT EVENTS

PRIDES

EARLY JUNE	Bushwick (Brooklyn) Pride
EARLY JUNE	Queens Pride (QUEENSPRIDE.COM)
EARLY JUNE	Staten Island Pride (SIHEALTHACTION.ORG)
MID JUNE	Brooklyn Pride (BROOKLYNPRIDE.ORG)
MID JUNE	Bronx Pride (BRONXPRIDE.ORG)
LATE JUNE	New York City Pride (NYCPRIDE.ORG)
	A huge roster of both official and independent events including the Blaque & White Ball, The Dyke March, Lincoln Center Salutes Gay Pride, and Stonewall Sails Regatta
AUGUST	Pride in the City (PRIDEINTHECITY.COM) NYC's largest black pride event

OTHER GAY-POPULAR EVENTS AND FESTIVALS

FEBRUARY	Fall Fashion Week (MBFASHIONWEEK.COM/NEWYORK)
MARCH	Armory Show (THEARMORYSHOW.COM)
LATE MAY	Fleet Week (FLEETWEEK.NAVY.MIL)
MAY–JUNE	NewFest, the NY LGBT Film Festival (NEWFEST.ORG)
LATE JUNE	Coney Island Mermaid Parade (CONEYISLAND.COM/MERMAID.SHTML)
AUGUST	New York International Fringe Festival (FRINGENYC.ORG)
SEPTEMBER	Spring Fashion Week (MBFASHIONWEEK.COM/NEWYORK)

| OCTOBER 31 | Village Halloween Parade (HALLOWEEN NYC.COM) |
| NOVEMBER | MIX NYC, the NY Queer Experimental Film Festival (MIXNYC.ORG) |

VITAL NYC INFO
GAY PUBLICATIONS

GAY CITY NEWS America's largest-circulation lesbian and gay newspaper, weekly *Gay City News* is free at many gay establishments and on some street corners in gay neighborhoods. GAYCITYNEWS.COM

GONYC The nation's most widely distributed free monthly lesbian magazine, *GoNYC*, is available at girl establishments citywide. GONYCMAGAZINE.COM

HX Short for *Homo Xtra,* one of the city's two free boy weekly magazines highlighting nightlife and culture, available at gay establishments across town. HX.COM

NEXT A free weekly magazine with witty and informed insight on the city's gay nightlife and culture, also available at gay establishments across town. NEXTMAGAZINE.COM

METROSOURCE Bimonthly glossy for fashionable gay NYC men. METROSOURCE.COM

NEW YORK BLADE Weekly newspaper for the city's gay and lesbian community, available at more than 900 locations around town. NYBLADE.COM

OTHER PUBLICATIONS

NEW YORK MAGAZINE A very informed and hip weekly publication geared especially at locals, but visitors can find great tips about what's going on around town. NYMAG.COM

NEW YORKER The grand dame of weekly local information excelling in the highbrow arena, with excellent prose and those cartoons you love. NEWYORKER.COM

NEW YORK TIMES A must-get for visitors, especially for its great Friday entertainment preview and its Sunday Arts & Leisure Roundup. NYTIMES.COM

TIME OUT NEW YORK Fantastic weekly newsstand resource with concise reviews of everything a visitor could possibly want to know about the local art, theater, music, dance, film, restaurant, and yes, even gay scenes. TIMEOUTNY.COM

GENERAL TOURISM INFO

NYC & COMPANY The city's official visitor information center. 810 Seventh Ave. (between 52nd and 53rd Sts.), NYCVISIT.COM

WALKING TOURS

Countless interesting tours are on offer in the city virtually every day of the year, many run by groups but just as many by unaffiliated but devoted and highly knowledgeable individuals. *Time Out New York* is a great resource for the weekly rundown.

BIG ONION WALKING TOURS Scads of daily tours on a wide variety of topics, including a gay one (that unfortunately never seems to get scheduled). 212-439-1090, BIGONION.COM

DOS & DON'TS FOR THE NYC VISITOR

DO use your peripheral vision when walking, especially when crossing the street, even if you have the light. New York's streets are the veins to its high energy heart, and all manner of activity therefore transpires on them in all directions at once. Bike messengers and shopping carts of recyclables tend not to pay much mind to traffic rules.

DO ride the subways. Yes, they're dirty, yes, you'll see and hear and smell all manner of things, but in all likelihood you will survive, and you'll be richer for the experience. And once you do it you'll be hooked, as it really is rather efficient.

DO try a pedicab. Despite Dave Letterman's teasing that they're just old bikes with milk crates hammered on the back, human-powered pedicabs are a quick and green way to get around the city, and offer a unique open-air NYC street ride you won't soon forget.

DO be prepared to step in dog poop. The streets are exponentially cleaner of the stuff than they were before curb laws, but random piles are everywhere. Carry portable wet naps for just such an occasion.

DO call DoITT (the Department of Information Technology and Telecommunications), better known as 311, the number set up by the city to handle all calls relating to nonemergency municipal services. Live staffers will answer any city-related question, 24 hours a day.

DON'T rent a car. There's really no need, and you'll be sorry.

DON'T overstay your welcome at your New York City friend's apartment. Space for the vast majority of city dwellers is extremely limited, and as much as they love you, it gets annoying to be stumbling over you, especially when you're vacationing while they're working. Sorry, but the fish/houseguest rule is pretty accurate: after three days, you stink.

DON'T stand in the middle of the sidewalk to check your map, read this book, or do anything else for that matter. Few things annoy New Yorkers more than people who don't use sidewalks for moving.

DON'T ride the subways late at night—not because they're more dangerous, but because they run too infrequently. There's nothing worse than waiting half an hour for a train with a bunch of rowdy drunks when you're just ready for bed. Spring for a cab and remind yourself that time is money.

DON'T ride in gypsy cabs, which are private cars roaming the city looking for fares; you may be approached by one

DOS & DON'TS FOR THE NYC VISITOR

at the airport or as you're waiting to hail a licensed yellow cab. While many of them are safe and honest, plenty are not, and it's simply not worth the risk, especially if you don't know where you're going.

DON'T be afraid to ask questions. Most New Yorkers are quite eager to help if you're lost, and only the most ruthless will knowingly point you in the wrong direction.

EAST VILLAGE WALKING TOURS Tuesday, Friday, and Saturday tours: basic, bar crawl, or gangsters, murderers, and weirdos. 917-215-2575, EAST-VILLAGE.COM/TOUR

GREENWICH VILLAGE LITERARY PUB CRAWL Get lit as you learn lit with this actor-guided Saturday afternoon tour of the Village. 212-613-5796, BAKERLOO.ORG/PUBCRAWL

SOCIAL SERVICES

GAY MEN'S HEALTH CRISIS Working to prevent and treat HIV, the GMHC responds to over 35,000 requests for support annually and has a referral bank of over 10,000 service providers. The Tisch Building, 119 West 24th St. (between Sixth and Seventh Aves.), 212-367-1000 or anonymous hotline 212-807-6655, GMHC.ORG

THE LESBIAN, GAY, BISEXUAL & TRANSGENDER COMMUNITY CENTER Providing a wide swath of services to virtually every sector of the gay community, The Center is also the meeting place of over 300 groups. 208 W. 13th St. (at Seventh Ave.), 212-620-7310, GAYCENTER.ORG

RECOVERY MEETINGS Info and links to 12-step addiction recovery meetings around the city for gay visitors to New York. ROYY.COM

CULTURAL ORGANIZATIONS

AUDRE LORDE PROJECT A lesbian, gay, bisexual, two spirit, trans, and gender nonconforming people of color center for community organizing, focusing on the New York City area. 85 S. Oxford St. (at Lafayette Ave.), 718-596-0342, Brooklyn, ALP.ORG

GALDE: GAY AND LESBIAN DOMINICAN EMPOWERMENT ORGANIZATION 24 W. 25th St. (between Broadway and Sixth Ave., 9th Floor), 718-596-0342 x39, GALDE.ORG

GAY AND LESBIAN ARAB SOCIETY GLAS.ORG/NYC

GAY MEN OF AFRICAN DESCENT 103 E. 125th St. (at Park Ave., Suite 503), 212-828-1697, GMAD.ORG
IRISH QUEERS 212-289-1101, IRISHQUEERS.ORG

LAS BUENAS AMIGAS LESBIANAS LATINAS EN NUEVA YORK 718-596-0342 x44, LASBUENASAMIGAS.ORG

LATINO GAY MEN OF NEW YORK 718-596-0342 x36 or 212-367-1092, LGMNY.ORG

MEN OF ALL COLORS TOGETHER/NEW YORK MACTNY.ORG

GREAT WEB SITES ABOUT NYC

BOYS IN THE SUN Candid photography of "street" boys in Manhattan. BOYSINTHESUN.BLOGSPOT.COM

CLUB FREETIME Scores of daily listings of free (or very cheap) things to do around the city, including readings, concerts, and walks. CLUBFREETIME.COM

CRASHSTAT Scare the bejeezus out of yourself before even getting here with this interactive map showing a street by street breakdown of the last decade or so of NYC pedestrian and bike accidents. Spoiler alert: There's been one at virtually every corner. CRASHSTAT.COM

CURBED This NYC blog is much watched by in-the-know locals for the latest neighborhood and real estate news. CURBED.COM

FORGOTTEN NY Great site chock full of tender morsels from the city's rich past that have been mostly overlooked by history. FORGOTTEN-NY.COM

GAWKER STALKER Much more civilized than L.A.'s paparazzi culture, New York tracks its celebrities (besides via the *New York Post's Page Six*, of course) through everyman tipsters sharing their recent sights on this site. GAWKER.COM/STALKER

GREAT WEB SITES ABOUT NYC

GOTHAMIST NYC's most popular local blog, reflecting, as the *New York Times* puts it, "everything worth knowing about this city." GOTHAMIST.COM

HISTORY OF GAY BARS IN NEW YORK CITY A unique, fascinating, and comprehensive look at the city's pink cocktail history, with special focus on early mafia control. BITTERQUEEN.TYPEPAD.COM

HOPSTOP Directions point to point using New York City's subway (and/or bus) system. HOPSTOP.COM

MENUPAGES An invaluable NYC restaurant screening tool, tracking nearly 6,500 restaurants in New York City through diner reviews. MENUPAGES.COM

NEW YORK CITY: A GAY HISTORY Basic but interesting site giving info on a host of locales from the gay history of Greenwich Village, Chelsea, and Times Square. GAYHISTORY.WEB1000.COM

NEW YORK SONGLINES Thousands of absolutely fascinating collected random history tidbits on NYC addresses, displayed block by block. NYC.RR.COM/JKN/NYSONGLINES

GREAT WEB SITES ABOUT NYC

OVERHEARD IN NEW YORK Conveying the utter randomness of New York City life, bizarre and often hilarious snippets of actual conversations shared by eavesdropping strangers. OVERHEARDINNEWYORK.COM

SAVORY NEW YORK Video guide to some of the city's top restaurants, featuring interviews with the people behind them. SAVORYNEWYORK.COM

SOUTH ASIAN LESBIAN GAY ASSOCIATION SALGA.ORG

FIERCE! (FABULOUS INDEPENDENT EDUCATED RADICALS FOR COMMUNITY EMPOWERMENT!) A community organization for transgender, lesbian, gay, bisexual, two spirit, queer, and questioning (TLGBTSQQ) youth of color in New York City. FIERCENYC.ORG

RELIGIOUS ORGANIZATIONS

CONGREGATION BETH SIMCHAT TORAH 57 Bethune St. (between Washington and West Sts.), West Village, 212-929-9498, CBST.ORG

DIGNITY NEW YORK 218 W. 11th St. (at Waverly Pl.), West Village, 646-418-7039, DIGNITYNY.ORG

METROPOLITAN COMMUNITY CHURCH OF NEW YORK 446 W. 36th St. (between Ninth and Tenth Aves.), Hell's Kitchen, 212-629-7440, MCCNY.ORG

NEW YORK CITY CHRISTIAN SCIENCE GROUP FOR THE LGBT COMMUNITY The Center, 208 W. 13th St. (at Seventh Ave.), West Village, 800-454-1906 x1299, NYCSGROUP.COM

GYMS

The city has hundreds of gyms from which to choose; these are a few of the top gay favorites.

CRUNCH Eight Manhattan locations, with Lafayette being especially gay popular. CRUNCH.COM

DAVID BARTON Most people's pick as the best gay gym in the city. Upper East Side location too, with Astor Place opening soon. 215 W. 23rd St. (between Seventh and Eighth Aves.), 212-414-2022, DAVIDBARTONGYM.COM

EQUINOX Eighteen Manhattan locations. EQUINOXFITNESS.COM

NEW YORK SPORTS CLUB Many locations, and here's a shocker: the 23rd St. and Eighth Ave. one in Chelsea is the gayest. MYSPORTSCLUBS.COM

SPAS

BODY BEAUTIFUL SPA Full service day spa and laser hair removal. 96 E. 7th St. (between First Ave. and Ave. A), East Village, BODYBEAUTIFULSPA.COM

FACE TO FACE NYC DAY SPA This popular spa offers much more than anal bleaching, the racy ad campaign for which brought it special attention recently. 20 W. 20th St. (between Fifth and Sixth Aves, Suite 603), 212-633-0404, Chelsea, FACETOFACENYC.COM

NICKEL SPA This big and very gay-popular spa was the first upscale men-only spot in town. 77 Eighth Ave. (at 14th St.), 212-242-3203, West Village/Chelsea, NICKELSPANYC.COM

SMOOTHMED Featuring that great gay dream, walk-in botox. 111 E. 59th St. (between Park and Lexington Aves.), Midtown, 212-371-SMOOTH (7666)

GAY SPORTS ORGANIZATIONS

BIG APPLE DODGEBALL (BAD) BIGAPPLEDODGEBALL.COM

BIG APPLE SOFTBALL LEAGUE BIGAPPLESOFTBALL.COM

BROOKLYN BLADES Women's ice hockey. BROOKLYNBLADES.ORG

FAST & FABULOUS New York's lesbian and gay cycling club. 212-567-7160, FASTNFAB.ORG

FRONT RUNNERS NEW YORK Hosts Pride Run. FRNY.ORG

HOT NUDE YOGA Naked gay men exploring tantra. HNY Studio, 100 W. 23 St., 4th floor (buzzer 4), HOTNUDEYOGA.COM

METRO GAY WRESTLING ALLIANCE METROWRESTLING.ORG

GOTHAM KNIGHTS RUGBY FOOTBALL CLUB GOTHAMRFC.ORG

GOTHAM VOLLEYBALL GOTHAMVOLLEYBALL.ORG

KNICKERBOCKER SAILING ASSOCIATION KSA-NYC.ORG

METROPOLITAN TENNIS GROUP METROTENNISGROUP.COM

NEW YORK CITY GAY BASKETBALL LEAGUE
NYCGAYBASKETBALL.ORG

NEW YORK CITY GAY HOCKEY ASSOCIATION 212-252-4351,
NYCGAYHOCKEY.ORG

NEW YORK GAY FOOTBALL LEAGUE NYGAYFOOTBALL.ORG

NEW YORK GAY POOL LEAGUE MEMBERS.AOL.COM/NYGPL/
POOL.HTM

NEW YORK RAMBLERS SOCCER CLUB
NEWYORKRAMBLERS.ORG

SKI BUMS New York City's club for gay and lesbian skiers and
snowboarders. SKI-BUMS.ORG

SUNDANCE OUTDOOR ADVENTURE SOCIETY
SUNDANCEOUTDOOR.ORG

TEAM NEW YORK AQUATICS Swimmers, water polo players, and
synchronists of all levels of experience. TNYA.ORG

NEW YORK CITY:
THE EPICENTER OF GAY CULTURE

No place in the world matches New York for its interdisciplinary blend of cultural dominance. As one of the globe's top hubs for art, dance, music, and theater, the city's a veritable fountain of high (and low) culture. And as we all know by now, with culture comes gays—and in New York's case, lots of them. Gay people make up such large contingents of virtually every one of NYC's cultural fields that the city's arts and gay histories are powerfully intertwined.

ART

Arguably (usually with Brits these days) the center of the art world, New York boasts several of its most important museums (listed later by neighborhood) and upward of 500 galleries, most of the biggest concentrated in Chelsea, but other strong players can be found in SoHo, Midtown, the Lower East Side, and Brooklyn's DUMBO neighborhood. While your best bets are below, for further exploration check out the Chelsea Gallery Map (CHELSEAGALLERYMAP.COM).

BEST BETS FOR ART GALLERIES

ANDREA ROSEN GALLERY Gallerist of art superstars past (including László Moholy-Nagy) and present (including Wolfgang

10 GREAT GAY ARTWORKS IN NYC MUSEUMS

DISTINGUISHED AIR Charles Demuth, 1930, Whitney Museum of American Art

FIRE David Wojnarowicz, 1987, Museum of Modern Art

KEN & TYLER Robert Mapplethorpe, 1985, Guggenheim Museum

JULIA MARTIN, JULIA BREDT AND SELF DRESSED UP AS MEN Alice Austen, 1891, Staten Island Historical Society

MUSICIANS Michelangelo Merisi da Caravaggio, 1595, Metropolitan Museum of Art

Tillmans), Andrea Rosen also has her eyes keenly peeled to the future. 525 W. 24th St. (between Tenth and Eleventh Aves., Chelsea map G1), 212-627-6000, ANDREAROSENGALLERY.COM

ARMORY SHOW Taking its name from the 1913 New York City exhibition that introduced modern art to America, the Armory Show has since its 1994 reincarnation grown into one of the country's most important art events, with key galleries and buyers from around the globe gathering on the Hell's Kitchen riverside every year in late March. Pier 54, Hell's Kitchen map G2, 212-645-6440, THEARMORYSHOW.COM

10 GREAT GAY ARTWORKS IN NYC MUSEUMS

PORTRAIT OF GERTRUDE STEIN Pablo Picasso, 1946, Metropolitan Museum of Art

SELF-PORTRAIT Sir Anthony van Dyck, possibly 1620–21, Metropolitan Museum of Art

TWO LOVERS Riza-i Abbasi, 1630, Metropolitan Museum of Art

UNTITLED from *Marilyn Monroe (Marilyn)* Andy Warhol, 1967, Museum of Modern Art

THE WARREN CUP 1st century, Metropolitan Museum of Art

DANIEL REICH GALLERY Everyone's pick for "the one to watch," the Daniel Reich Gallery hosts hot emerging artists like gay culture fun-poker Christian Holstad. 537A W. 23rd St. (between Tenth and Eleventh Aves., Chelsea map G3), 212-924-4949, DANIELREICHGALLERY.COM

DEITCH PROJECTS Quirky con capital Q and queer-friendly to boot, Deitch Projects puts on some of the city's hippest shows and related events, with strong ties to the Fischerspooner/Dazzle Dancer world of downtown art-fag fabulousness. In September they host the ultrafab Art Parade that turns SoHo's West Broadway

IN THE STEPS OF PAUL CADMUS

Paul Cadmus may have been one of the world's first openly gay artists, but he shied away from ever being revered for such a thing. Born in 1904 to artist parents on the Upper West Side, Cadmus rose to overnight fame in 1934 when his homoerotically turbo-charged painting *The Fleet's In!*, commissioned by the Public Works of Art Project (a Roosevelt-era New Deal initiative), so upset Navy hotshots for its depiction of lurid sexuality that they seized it from the Washington, D.C., gallery where it was hanging. Ironically the painting now resides at The Navy Museum, where it's among the more popular attractions.

Cadmus enjoyed a highly successful career in the ensuing years, working for 25 of those from his studio at **5 ST. LUKE'S** (between Hudson St. and Seventh Ave. South, Greenwich Village map P2), where his list of illustrious gay

into a sea of creative craziness. 76 Grand St. (between Greene and Wooster Sts., SoHo map G4), 212.343.7300, DEITCH.COM

LESLIE/LOHMAN GALLERY The culmination of decades of collecting by founders Fritz Lohman and Charles Leslie, this large gallery is the showplace of the important Leslie/Lohman Gay Art Foundation and celebrates artists with the bravery to embrace a queer aesthetic. 26 Wooster St. (between Grand and Canal Sts.), SoHo (map G5), 212-431-2609, LESLIELOHMAN.ORG

IN THE STEPS OF PAUL CADMUS

visitors included Tennessee Williams, Andy Warhol, and E. M. Forster. "It was quite easy to be [gay] in the Village," told Cadmus of that era to author Daniel Hurewitz, as relayed in his book *Stepping Out: Nine Walks Through New York City's Gay and Lesbian Past.* "It wasn't much of a problem, but one was secretive. You could get into trouble."

Though the great majority of Cadmus's subsequent work focused on homages to the male form (many featuring his partner of 35 years, Jon Anderson) and had clear gay allure, Cadmus himself often dismissed the focus on homosexuality. "It's not so interesting to be gay," he told Hurewitz. In 1980, filmmaker David Sutherland profiled the groundbreaking painter in *Paul Cadmus: Enfant Terrible at 80,* which was broadcast nationally on PBS. Cadmus died in Weston, Connecticut, in 1999, just five days shy of his 95th birthday.

MARIAN GOODMAN GALLERY Known for a megastar flock of international contemporary artists that includes Jeff Wall and Steve McQueen, Marian Goodman is one of the city's most revered dealers. 24 W. 57th St., 212-977-7160, MARIANGOODMAN.COM

MATTHEW MARKS GALLERY Art powerhouse Matthew Marks boasts Nan Goldin, Brice Mardin, Jasper Johns, and Ellsworth Kelly as members of his assembly. 523 W. 24th St. (between Tenth and Eleventh Aves., Chelsea map G7), 212-243-0200, MATTHEWMARKS.COM

CLUBS

Keeping on top of New York's ever-evolving club scene is hard enough for locals, let alone for the sometime visitor. Since club nights change venues and names at breakneck speed, your best bet for a quick catch up is to check in with the personalities behind some of the most popular hits of the recent past, who are sure to be bringing more goodness under a different guise in the future. Note that while these are all gay-slanted promoters, there are plenty of excellent straight/mixed clubs out there as well. You're on your own in finding those, though watching *Time Out New York*'s weekly Clubs section is a good place to start.

BEST BETS FOR CLUBS

CHIP DUCKETT Promoter of long-running Pop Rocks! Thursdays and 1984 at Pyramid. SPINCYCLENYC.COM

DANIEL NARDICIO Wildly successful sleazefests for naughty hipsters. DLIST.COM

EARL DAX The genius behind the fabulous annual cabaret slate Weimar New York and such innovative clubs as Unisex Salon. EARLDAX.COM or SCENEDOWNTOWN.COM

JOHN BLAIR Former promoter of Roxy Saturdays. JBLAIR.COM

JOHNNY DYNELL AND CHI CHI VALENTI/MOTHER NYC The men behind club institutions Mother, Jackie 60, and Mr. Black. MOTHERNYC.COM

JONNY MCGOVERN "Gay pimp" and comedian hosts homo events all around town. MYSPACE.COM/JONNYMCGOVERN

JOSH WOOD Promoter of former fave Bank and the current Sebastian. MYSPACE.COM/JOSHWOODPRODUCTIONS

LARRY TEE Longtime promoter, DJ, and musician on the constant cusp of the next, and the brains behind Electroclash. MYSPACE.COM/NYLARRYTEE

MICHAEL FORMIKA JONES Hip promoter about town has the key to the Boysroom. MYSPACE.COM/AREA10018

BEST MULTICULTURE CLUBS

CURRY CLUB Indo-Caribbean happening. CURRYCLUBNYC.COM

DESILICIOUS/SHOLAY PRODUCTIONS Monthly queer South Asian events. SHOLAYEVENTS.COM

HABIBI Very popular club nights for gay Arabs. IZMIX.COM or MYSPACE.COM/NYCHABIBI

KRASH Queens-born hip-hop/salsa party. KRASHNYC.COM

BEST COUNTRY CLUB

BIG APPLE RANCH Country-western dance lessons and party every Saturday night. BIGAPPLERANCH.COM

BEST WOMEN'S CLUBS

GIRLNATION Established Saturday girl fave. MYSPACE.COM/GIRLNATIONNYC

NIKKI'S REMIX Friday club with diverse and friendly female crowd. NIKKISREMIX.COM

3

IN THE STEPS OF JEROME ROBBINS

Closeted, a McCarthy-era commie squealer, and perhaps most scandalous of all, active on—gasp—*Broadway,* Jerome Robbins may not seem like the ultimate gay representative of New York City's dance world, but his contribution to the development of the city's ballet scene was undeniably majorly important, and the man was undeniably (despite his own denials) gay. Born on New York's Lower East Side in 1918, Robbins (then Rabinowitz) was the son of Russian Jewish immigrants who raised him mostly in New Jersey. He was attracted to dance early, and by age 21 he had begun dancing in the choruses of a string of Broadway shows.

Robbins's first major attempt at choreography, *Fancy Free,* was a major event in American ballet history, introducing the world in 1944 not only to Robbins but also to composer Leonard Bernstein and set designer Oliver Smith. Ironically *Fancy Free* was inspired by Robbins's reaction to the flagrantly gay painting *The Fleet's In!* by Paul Cadmus (see In the Steps of Paul Cadmus, Art section, chapter 3), a reaction he later claimed not very convincingly was a negative one. "I inwardly rejected [the painting] though it gave me the idea of doing the ballet," he told the *Christian Science Monitor.* "I watched sailors, and girls, too, all over town. I wanted to show that the boys in the service are healthy, vital boys: there is nothing sordid or morbid about them." Indeed, by all accounts Robbins found nothing sordid nor morbid about healthy, vital boys, though he refused to ever admit his homosexuality.

Robbins became a founding member of the New York

IN THE STEPS OF JEROME ROBBINS

City Ballet at its inception in 1948 and its artistic director the following year, a post he would keep for more than 40 years. Meanwhile he rose to wider public acclaim for his choreography work on Broadway shows, most notably 1957's *West Side Story,* which he conceived, choreographed, and directed. He followed this up with 1959's *Gypsy.*

The black mark on Robbins's legacy would be his cooperation with Joseph McCarthy's House Committee on Un-American Activities, naming names of eight colleagues as Communist Party members in 1953, a move that saved him from blacklisting (very probably over his suspected homosexuality), but a move he reportedly deeply regretted later.

In 1997 Robbins finished the ballet *Brandenburg,* his 66th, for the City Ballet, and announced during its rehearsals that he felt he had one more big ballet in him. He would die the following year without letting that ballet—or his secret—out.

SHESCAPE Hot girl parties. SHESCAPE.COM

SNAPSHOT Very popular Tuesday rocker dyke party. SNAPSHOTNYC.COM or WWW.MYSPACE.COM/SNAPSHOTNYC

STARLETTE SUNDAY Chic gal affair boasting one of the city's most gorgeous mixed/femme clienteles. STARLETTESUNDAY.COM or MYSPACE.COM/STARLETTESUNDAY

DANCE

When it comes to the art of human movement, New York City is firmly footed at the world's forefront, home to both top modern companies like Trisha Brown and dance classics like the New York City Ballet, as well as a host of nonaffiliated but extremely talented upstart choreographers and performers. To see what's on when you're in town, check the *Village Voice* for modern listings and the *New Yorker* for classical.

BEST BETS FOR DANCE

BAM (BROOKLYN ACADEMY OF MUSIC) Now a century old and stronger than ever, BAM and its gorgeous Howard Gilman Opera House and smaller Harvey Theatre continue to host a staggering parade of performers, having already included everyone from Isadora Duncan to Bill T. Jones to Matthew Bourne. Every Memorial Day weekend BAM hosts the DanceAfrica Festival, and in the fall comes the kinetic Next Wave Festival. There's even a BAMbus to whisk you from Manhattan and back. 30 Lafayette Ave. (between Ashland Pl. and St. Felix St., Fort Greene, Brooklyn map C1), 718-636-4100, BAM.ORG

CITY CENTER The pre-Lincoln Center home to the New York City Ballet, City Center still hosts annual slates by Alvin Ailey, Paul Taylor, and the American Ballet Theatre, as well as the always exciting international hodgepodge program Fall for Dance in late September. 131 W. 55th St. (between Sixth and Seventh Aves., Midtown map C2), 212-581-1212, NYCITYCENTER.ORG

DANCE THEATER WORKSHOP DTW hosts one of the city's most consistently interesting rosters of contemporary work, highlighting New York–based choreographers but also showcasing international talents. Bessie Schönberg Theater, 219 W. 19th St. (between Seventh and Eighth Aves., Chelsea map C3), 212-691-6500, DTW.ORG

JOAN WEILL CENTER FOR DANCE The largest dedicated space for dance in the country, this amazing eight-story facility opened in 2004 and houses the esteemed Alvin Ailey American Dance Theater as well as the Ailey School. 405 W. 55th St. (at Ninth Ave., Hell's Kitchen map C4), 212-405-9000, ALVINAILEY.ORG

JOYCE THEATER Housed in a one-time gay porn house, the Joyce presents an exciting array of modern dance in an intimate setting. 175 Eighth Ave. (at 17th St., Chelsea map C5), 212-242-0800, JOYCE.ORG

THE KITCHEN With a history born of the performance art likes of Laurie Anderson, The Kitchen presents some of the most experimental dance work to be found in the city. 512 W. 19th St. (between Tenth and Eleventh Aves., Chelsea map C6), 212-255-5793, THEKITCHEN.ORG

NEW YORK STATE THEATER This magnificent Lincoln Center building is home to the New York City Ballet, famously molded by George Balanchine and in recent years invigorated by dancer/choreographer Christopher Wheeldon. Columbus Ave. at W. 63rd St. (Upper West Side map A5), 212-875-5000, LINCOLNCENTER.ORG

FILM

Unless you're in town for a festival, seeing a film may not be high on your list of things to do in New York City. But with some of the country's most inventive indie houses programming works sometimes rarely seen elsewhere, the city's a film lover's dreamland.

10 GREAT FILMIC TAKES ON GAY NYC

ANGELS IN AMERICA **(2003)** The HBO production of Tony Kushner's phenomenal play.

BEFORE STONEWALL **(1984)** Rita Mae Brown–narrated documentary recapping important events in gay and lesbian history before the infamous riots.

***CRUISING* (1980)** Highly controversial during its filming and initial release, this intense story of a cop (Al Pacino) who goes undercover on New York's leather scene to find a serial murderer has been given a mostly positive critical rethinking of late.

GAY SEX IN THE 70S **(2005)** A fascinating documentary look at NYC gay life in the decadent decade between Stonewall and AIDS.

LONGTIME COMPANION **(1990)** This touching NYC-set film was the first

Besides, at some point even you could use a couple hours off from the fast pace of the city.

BEST BETS FOR FILM

ANTHOLOGY FILM ARCHIVES Programs American independent and avant-garde cinema and its Euro/Soviet/Japanese precursors, and also hosts the annual New York Underground Film Festival in early spring. 32 Second Ave. (at E. 2nd St., East Village map F1), 212-505-5181, ANTHOLOGYFILMARCHIVES.ORG

10 GREAT FILMIC TAKES ON GAY NYC

mainstream release to deal with the AIDS crisis.

***MIDNIGHT COWBOY* (1969)** Joe Buck (Jon Voight) and Ratso Rizzo (Dustin Hoffman) are two moving misfits thrown together by the pressures of big city life.

***PARIS IS BURNING* (1990)** A fascinating docu-look at Harlem's drag ball culture.

***THE RITZ* (1976)** Straight Clevelander on the run from mobster brother-in-law hides in Manhattan gay bathhouse, and hilarity ensues.

***SHORT BUS* (2006)** John Cameron Mitchell's sexier take on sex and the city that finally reveals why people move to New York: to get fucked.

***TORCH SONG TRILOGY* (1988)** The film version of Harvey Fierstein's hit play costars Matthew Broderick and was an early gay-themed mainstream hit.

BAMCINÉMATEK Presents repertory classics, retrospectives, festivals, premieres, and rare screenings. BAM Rose Cinemas, 30 Lafayette Avenue (between Ashland Pl. and St. Felix St., Fort Greene, Brooklyn map F2), 718-636-4100, BAM.ORG/EVENTS/BAMCINEMATEK.ASPX

BRYANT PARK SUMMER FILM FESTIVAL A wildly popular local summer pastime, this free Monday evening film series shows some of the best-loved classics in the park. (Sixth Avenue between W. 40th

GREAT GAY NYC TV

Surely you didn't come to New York to watch television, but if you live here or if you're staying with friends who have cable access, a few shows are definitely worth checking out. Show times vary, but most run late night on MNN (Manhattan Neighborhood Network) or MNN2. For more info go to MNN.ORG

GAY ACTION NEWS Gay-slanted comedy news. MYSPACE.COM/GAYACTIONNEWS

MEN FOR MEN Robin Byrd's classic clips of male strippers, mostly from the '80s, making it almost as interesting culturally as it is carnally. Just be ready for the commercials, where she-males reveal all. ROBINBYRD.COM

OUT AND ABOUT Ryan and Rafael explore gay New York. MYSPACE.COM/MYNEWYORK

STRANGE FRUITS/ FRUTA EXTRAÑA The Bronx's own long-running high camp drag melodrama. STRANGEFRUITS.TV

and 42nd Sts., Midtown map F3), BRYANTPARK.ORG/CALENDAR/FILM-FESTIVAL.PHP

FILM FORUM A fantastic nonprofit revival and first-run independent cinematheque. 209 W. Houston St. (between Sixth Ave. and Varick St., West Village map F4), 212-727-8110, FILMFORUM.COM

IFC CENTER An offshoot of the Independent Film Channel, this is one of the city's best current-run indie film venues. It also hosts NewFest at IFC, a monthly series of past favorites from the gay film festival, specially curated programs, and local shorts (more info at newfest.org). 323 Sixth Ave. (at W. 3rd St., West Village map F5), 212-924-7771, IFCCENTER.COM

LANDMARK SUNSHINE CINEMA Another of the city's top current-run indie film theaters. 143 E. Houston St. (between Forsyth and Eldridge Sts., Lower East Side map F6), 212-330-8182, LANDMARKTHEATRES.COM/MARKET/NEWYORK/SUNSHINE CINEMA.HTM

MIX NYC: THE NEW YORK QUEER EXPERIMENTAL FILM FESTIVAL Edgy and always provocative lineup of homoflicks, held every November. MIXNYC.ORG

NEWFEST Now 20 years old, New York's biggest annual LGBT film festival is one of the country's most watched, and happens early in June. NEWFEST.ORG

QUEER BLACK CINEMA A monthly screening series of black gay films, held at The LGBT Community Center. QUEERBLACK CINEMA.COM

TRIBECA FILM FESTIVAL The city's most important high-profile cinematic event, held annually on the cusp of April and May. 212-941-2100, TRIBECAFILMFESTIVAL.ORG

TWO BOOTS PIONEER THEATER Showing a heady hodgepodge of independent and foreign films as well as innovative special series,

10 GREAT LITERARY TAKES ON GAY NYC

ART AND SEX IN GREENWICH VILLAGE: A MEMOIR OF GAY LITERARY LIFE AFTER STONEWALL **BY FELICE PICANO** An inside look back at the creative flurry that transpired in the gay lit world in the 1970s and '80s.

COLLECTED POEMS 1947–1997 **BY ALLEN GINSBERG** The works of the dearly departed gay Beat great.

THE COLLECTED POEMS OF FRANK O'HARA The provocative works of the NYC-based gay poet whose life was cut tragically short by a 1966 Fire Island dune buggy accident.

THE COLLECTED POEMS OF LANGSTON HUGHES The bold and brilliant works of the Harlem Renaissance man.

DRY: A MEMOIR **BY AUGUSTEN BURROUGHS** With brutal wit, gay lit fave Burroughs recounts his descent from NYC ad exec to alcoholic crackhead, and his subsequent rough climb toward recovery.

LEAVES OF GRASS: THE ORIGINAL 1855 EDITION **BY WALT WHITMAN** Before all the revisions, this was the luminous work that started it all for Whitman and the world.

MY LIFE AND THE PARADISE GARAGE: KEEP ON DANCIN' **BY MEL CHEREN** The "Godfather of Disco"

10 GREAT LITERARY TAKES ON GAY NYC

recounts his wild experiences in the disco creational 1970s, then the brutal aftermath of the AIDS–decimated '80s.

THE NEW YORK DIARY BY NED ROREM Fascinating firsthand account of the gay composer's life among the city's elite in the 1950s and early '60s.

ONE OF THE CHILDREN: GAY BLACK MEN IN HARLEM BY WILLIAM HAWKESWOOD A posthumously published study of the gay African American experience in Harlem and "the often uneasy fusion of race and sexuality in a country with a long and tortured history of segregation and bigotry on both counts."

ZAMI, A NEW SPELLING OF MY NAME BY AUDRE LORDE In what she called a "biomythography," eminent lesbian poet Lorde powerfully recounts her life experiences in Harlem and Greenwich Village.

Two Boots Pioneer Theater is, says *Salon,* "doing the movie gods' work on earth." 155 E. 3rd St. (between Aves. A and B, East Village map F7), 212-591-0434, TWOBOOTS.COM/PIONEER

LITERARY

New York City has served as the backdrop and/or inspiration for countless literary classics, including the works of a stream of gay icons from Walt Whitman to Langston Hughes to Allen Ginsberg to Michael Cunningham. Virtually every day of the year a full roster of good literary events awaits, from prose readings by established authors to experimental poetry by undiscovered geniuses.

BEST BETS FOR POETRY AND READINGS

These venues are among the best gay and gay-friendly readings spots in the city.

BLUESTOCKINGS 172 Allen St. (between Stanton and Rivington Sts.), Lower East Side, 212-777-6028, BLUESTOCKINGS.COM

OSCAR WILDE MEMORIAL BOOKSHOP, CHRISTOPHER STREET

BOWERY POETRY CLUB 308 Bowery (between Bleecker and Houston Sts.), East Village, 212-614-0505, BOWERYPOETRY.COM

HUE-MAN BOOKSTORE 2319 Frederick Douglass Blvd./Eighth Ave., Harlem, 212-665-7400, HUEMANBOOKSTORE.COM

92ND STREET Y 1395 Lexington Ave. (between 91st and 92nd Sts.), Upper East Side, 212-415-5500, 92Y.ORG

OSCAR WILDE BOOKSHOP 15 Christopher St. (at Gay St.), West Village, 212-255-8097, OSCARWILDEBOOKS.COM

RAPTURE CAFÉ & BOOKS 200 Ave. A (between 12th and 13th Sts.), East Village, 212-228-1177, RAPTURECAFE.COM

THREE LIVES & COMPANY 154 W. 10 St. (at Waverly Pl.), West Village, 212-741-2069, THREELIVES.COM

MUSIC

Musically speaking, New York City is both a haven for the highbrow classics and a hotbed of upstart indie bands—and in between, virtually every flavor of music imaginable, represented nightly at venues all across the city. Your best bets for those listings are the *Village Voice* and *Time Out New York,* though *New York* and the *New Yorker* are also good.

BEST BETS FOR CLASSICAL MUSIC

CARNEGIE HALL One of the country's most famous and beloved venues, Carnegie Hall presents around 100 performances per season (fall to spring). W. 57th St. (at Seventh Ave., Midtown map M1), 212-247-7800, CARNEGIEHALL.ORG

IN THE STEPS OF GLADYS BENTLEY

It's hard to grasp the groundbreaking scope of the Harlem Renaissance until you know singer Gladys Bentley, the 250-pound cross-dressing lesbian who saw enormous success in the 1920s and '30s playing speakeasies and clubs like Ubangi, where she was reportedly backed by a chorus line of drag queens. Born in 1907 in Philadelphia, Bentley came to New York at 16 and settled in Harlem, where her powerful voice and shameless embrace of her sexuality made her a huge sensation. She dressed in men's clothes almost exclusively, flirted aggressively with female audience members, and at one point told a gossip columnist that she'd married a white woman in Atlantic City. In their books of the period, several writers of the Renaissance movement (including Carl Van Vechten) based characters on Bentley's unique presence.

With the decline of the Renaissance's fervor, in 1937 Bentley moved to Los Angeles to live with her mother. She seems to have had a lesbian following at shows that she played both in L.A. and San Francisco, but with the rise of McCarthy-era antihomosexuality, began separating herself from lesbianism. In the early '50s she told *Ebony* magazine that she'd been cured of her attraction to women via female hormone treatments, and she appeared in photos wearing a dress and cleaning house for her new husband, who she eventually divorced. She continued singing at Hollywood clubs, and appeared on Groucho Marx's *You Bet Your Life* TV show twice. In 1960, she succumbed during a flu epidemic at age 52.

10 GREAT MUSICAL TAKES ON GAY NYC

Put these on your iPod and stay happy on the subway under all manner of nefarious conditions.

AUTUMN IN NEW YORK Billie Holiday

THE LUCKIEST GUY ON THE LOWER EAST SIDE Magnetic Fields

NATIVE NEW YORKER Odyssey

NEW YORK CITY BOY Pet Shop Boys

NEW YORK I LOVE YOU LCD Soundsystem

NEW YORK, NEW YORK Liza Minnelli

NEW YORK, NEW YORK Nina Hagen

SODA SHOP Jay Brannan

WAKE UP IN NEW YORK Craig Armstrong with Evan Dando

WALK ON THE WILD SIDE Lou Reed

LINCOLN CENTER FOR THE PERFORMING ARTS The magnificent jewel in the city's artistic crown, Lincoln Center hosts the Metropolitan Opera, the New York Opera, the New York Philharmonic, and the Chamber Music Society. Columbus Ave., W. 62nd to 65th Sts., (Upper West Side map A5), 212-875-5000, LINCOLNCENTER.ORG

MILLER THEATRE Columbia University's Miller Theatre presents works from world-class musicians, from fall through spring. 2960 Broadway (at 116th St., Harlem map M3), 212-854-7799, MILLERTHEATER.COM

10 GREAT GAY PERFORMERS YOU SHOULD SEE IN NYC

If you notice that any of these top acts on the NYC scene are singing/dancing/DJing/showing/appearing around town during your stay, get there to see them.

Creation Nation	Linda Simpson
Dazzle Dancers	Murray Hill
Flotilla DeBarge	Lady Bunny
Jay Brannan	Sherry Vine
Justin Bond/Kiki & Herb	Sweetie

BEST BETS FOR POP MUSIC

BOWERY BALLROOM The Bowery hosts some of the hottest local and touring alternative faves. 6 Delancey St. (between Bowery and Chrystie St., Lower East Side map M4), 212-533-2111, BOWERYBALLROOM.COM

HIGHLINE BALLROOM The city's newest pop music palace, the Highline serves as a main venue for the annual High Line Festival. 431 W. 16th St. (between Ninth and Tenth Aves., Chelsea map M5), 212-414-5994, HIGHLINEBALLROOM.COM

JOE'S PUB In 10 brief years, nonprofit Joe's Pub has become a city institution, having hosted such far-flung legends as Elvis Costello, Dolly Parton, Laurie Anderson, and Kiki & Herb. 425 Lafayette St. (between 4th St. and Astor Pl., East Village map M6), 212-967-7555, JOESPUB.COM

MUSIC HALL OF WILLIAMSBURG This conversion of the former Northsix space now hosts indie music delights. 66 N. 6th St. (between Kent and Wythe Sts., Williamsburg, Brooklyn map M7), 212-260-4700, MUSICHALLOFWILLIAMSBURG.COM

WEBSTER HALL Once a speakeasy and a drag ball venue, Webster Hall now presents a streaming roster of alt-music darlings. 125 E. 11th St. (between Second and Third Aves., East Village map M8), 212-353-1600, WEBSTERHALL.COM

THEATER

No place in the world (hush, Londoners) is better known for its theater than New York City, with Broadway creating most of the hype. New shows come and go all the time, so we can't possibly list them for you here. Your best bets for up-to-the-minute listings and reviews are the weekly *New York, New Yorker,* and *Time Out New York* magazines, and the Friday and Sunday editions of the *New York Times.* The Web site NYTHEATRE.COM is another invaluable resource for all manner of NYC theater.

BEST BETS FOR OFF- AND OFF-OFF-BROADWAY THEATER AND PERFORMANCE

These venues offer consistently excellent shows, many of them with gay themes.

ACTORS PLAYHOUSE Long a venue for gay theater, and known for such past hits as *Naked Boys Singing* and *My Big Gay Italian Wedding.* 100 Seventh Ave. South (at Grove St., West Village map T1), 212-463-0060

3

GREAT (AND NOT SO GREAT) MOMENTS IN GAY NYC THEATER HISTORY

1896 The play *A Florida Enchantment* opens at Hoyt's Theatre (24th St., at Broadway), and for the first time on an American stage features two women kissing; at intermission ushers offer ice water to patrons who feel faint.

1923 Police arrest the theater owner, the producer, and twelve cast members of the Broadway show *The God of Vengeance* at the Apollo Theatre (223 W. 42nd St., between Seventh and Eighth Aves.) for "presenting an obscene, indecent, immoral and impure theatrical production," despite the fact it had already appeared without incident in nine European countries.

1926 Riding on the success of her racy first Broadway play *Sex,* Mae West visits popular gay cabaret showplace Paul & Joe's (62 W. 9th St., between Fifth and Sixth Aves.) to research her upcoming play *The Drag,* and reportedly auditions fifty men she meets there. Horrified authorities rush to shut down *Sex* and arrest West before *The Drag* can make it to Broadway.

1927 To silence a barrage of plays "depicting or dealing with the subject of sex degeneracy or sex perversion" on the New York stage, the Wales Padlock Law is enacted; one of its first victims is the lesbian love

GREAT (AND NOT SO GREAT) MOMENTS IN GAY NYC THEATER HISTORY

drama *The Captive,* which had been showing at the Empire Theatre (1430 Broadway at 40th St.).

1968 *The Boys in the Band* opens at Theatre Four (424 W. 55th St., between Ninth and Tenth Aves.), where it will run for 1,000 shows and spawns a 1970 movie, the first to focus on queer culture.

1969 Katherine Hepburn stars as Coco Chanel in the musical *Coco,* which opens at the Mark Hellinger Theatre (237 W. 51st St., between Broadway and Eighth Ave.) and purportedly features the first openly gay character in a Broadway musical, the despicable designer Sebastian Baye (played by René Auberjonois, whose performance won him a Tony).

1970 Based on the screenplay for *All About Eve,* the Lauren Bacall vehicle *Applause* opens at the Palace Theatre (1564 Broadway, between 46th and 47th Sts.) and features the character of hairdresser Duane (Lee Roy Reams), by all accounts the first likeable openly gay presence in a Broadway musical.

1975 Reimagining what a Fred Astaire/Ginger Rogers '30s musical could've been like if gay love had been accepted then, *Boy Meets Boy* opens at the 13th Street

GREAT (AND NOT SO GREAT) MOMENTS IN GAY NYC THEATER HISTORY

Repertory Company (50 W. 13th St., between Fifth and Sixth Aves.), becoming the first musical written by gays for gays to attract mainstream attention.

1982 The first of 1,222 Broadway performances of Harvey Fierstein's *Torch Song Trilogy* (which will go on to take the 1983 Tony Award for Best Play) begins at the Little Theatre (240 W. 44th St., between Seventh and Eighth Aves.).

1984 Charles Busch's *Vampire Lesbians of Sodom* is first performed at the Limbo Lounge (647 E. 9th St., between Aves. B and C), and will go on to be one of the longest-running plays in Off-Broadway history.

1993 Tony Kushner's *Angels in America: A Gay Fantasia on National Themes* has its Broadway debut at the Walter Kerr Theatre (219 W. 48th St., between Broadway and Eighth Ave.); its two halves, *Millennium Approaches* and *Perestroika,* win back-to-back Best Play Tonys in 1993 and 1994.

FRINGENYC Also known by its longer name, The New York International Fringe Festival, FringeNYC is an annual two-weeks-in-August slate of some of the edgiest new works by up-and-coming artists, featuring over 200 companies working in a variety of formats. FRINGENYC.ORG

NEW YORK THEATRE WORKSHOP Renowned for its diverse productions of important new works, this is where *Rent* got its start. 79 E. 4th St. (between Bowery and Second Ave., East Village map T2), 212-460-5475, NYTW.ORG

P.S. 122 One of the city's and the country's premier venues for performance art and innovative theater, former public school Performance Space 122 has hosted such alt-gay faves as Tim Miller and Ron Athey. 150 First Ave. (at E. 11th St., East Village map T3), 212-477-5288, PSI22.ORG

RADIO CITY MUSIC HALL

PUBLIC THEATER The Joseph Papp-founded Public was where both *Hair* and *A Chorus Line* debuted, and it still presents some of the most exciting new work in the city, not least of which being the emerging-talent-showcasing Under the Radar festival it hosts every January. It also operates the cabaret-ish Joe's Pub and Central Park's Delacorte Theater, which hosts the hugely popular (and free) star-studded Shakespeare in the Park series every summer. 425 Lafayette St. (between Astor Pl. and E. 4th St., East Village map T4), 212-539-8900, PUBLICTHEATER.COM

ZIPPER FACTORY THEATRE Housed in—surprise—a former garment district zipper factory, this complex of theater, tavern, and three bars hosts some of the most exciting entertainment in town, including gay and gay-popular acts like Margaret Cho, Lypsinka, Murray Hill, Scissor Sisters, and Jay Brannan. 336 W. 37th St. (between Eighth and Ninth Aves., Hell's Kitchen map T5), 212-352-3101, ZIPPERTHEATER.COM

BEST BETS FOR CHEAP BROADWAY TICKETS

With seats for most Broadway shows topping out at over $100 these days, poking about for available discounts can definitely be worth your while.

BROADWAYBOX.COM Serves up a veritable bonanza of discount codes for nearly every show. BROADWAYBOX.COM

CARE-TIX/BROADWAY CARES For a contribution equal to (and on top of) the ticket price, Care-Tix/Broadway Cares can pull strings to get you entertainment industry (i.e., good) seats, even to sold-out shows. 212-840-0770 (ask for Care-Tix)

NYTHEATRE.COM Offers some great "virtual coupons," mostly for smaller shows. NYTHEATRE.COM/NYTHEATRE/VC.HTM

TKTS Queue early the day of the show at TKTS for up to 50% off seats that are sometimes excellent. Its futuristically renovated Duffy Square location is scheduled for completion in June 2008. Until then, the temporary spot is the Marriott Marquis Hotel, W. 46th St. (between Broadway and 8th Ave.), Midtown, TDF.ORG/TKTS

3

NEW YORK CITY: THE EPICENTER OF GAY CULTURE

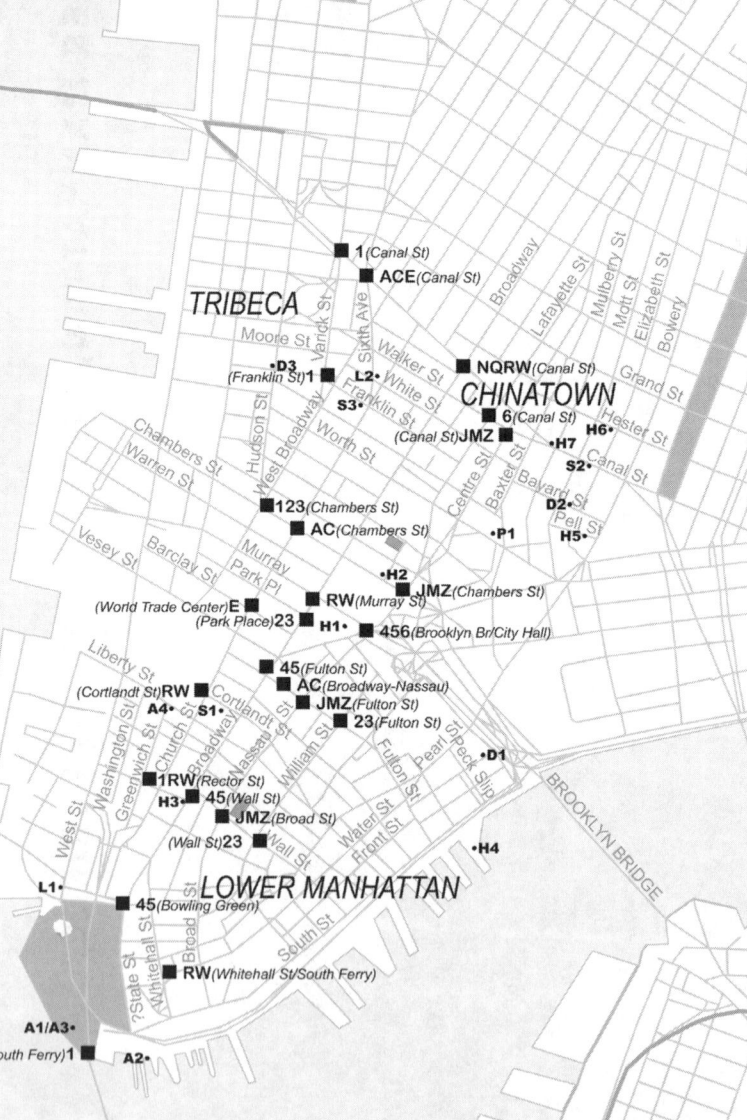

TRIBECA

CHINATOWN

LOWER MANHATTAN

1 *(Canal St)*
ACE *(Canal St)*

•D3
*(Franklin St)*1
L2•
S3•
NQRW *(Canal St)*
6 *(Canal St)*
*(Canal St)*JMZ
H6•
•H7
S2•
123 *(Chambers St)*
AC *(Chambers St)*
•P1
D2•
H5•
•H2
JMZ *(Chambers St)*
*(World Trade Center)*E
RW *(Murray St)*
*(Park Place)*23
H1•
456 *(Brooklyn Br/City Hall)*
45 *(Fulton St)*
*(Cortlandt St)*RW
AC *(Broadway-Nassau)*
A4•
S1•
JMZ *(Fulton St)*
23 *(Fulton St)*
•D1
1RW *(Rector St)*
H3•
45 *(Wall St)*
JMZ *(Broad St)*
*(Wall St)*23
•H4
45 *(Bowling Green)*
L1•
RW *(Whitehall St/South Ferry)*
A1/A3•
*(South Ferry)*1
A2•

BROOKLYN BRIDGE

LOWER MANHATTAN

This relatively small area south of Chambers Street and the Brooklyn Bridge is where it all began. His successor Peter Minuit hogs all the credit, but we owe a lot to Willem Verhulst, who in 1625 as director of the Dutch West India Company decided that Manhattan was the optimal place in New Netherlands for permanent settlement. We've been permanently settling ever since.

Yes, this is the bustling modern home of Wall Street and the Financial District, but it's also the place where New York City life—and therefore New York City gay life—got its start. Centuries of progress and repeated rebuilding haven't left a lot of evidence of that history, but somehow it's all still here in the air.

Of course more than any other area, Lower Manhattan is emblazoned on the modern public consciousness as symbolic of New York City, having been the site of the September 11, 2001 terrorist attacks. Tragic and difficult as they were to bear, those attacks did not bring down Lower Manhattan, and moreover they've managed to instill it—and frankly the entire city—with renewed vigor ever since.

LOWER MANHATTAN GAY TIMELINE

1660 Twenty-four-year-old New Amsterdam colony soldier and newlywed Jan Guisthout van der Linden is tied in a sack and drowned for sodomizing his manservant, who is also summarily whipped for his involvement.

1701 Edward Hyde (Lord Cornbury), nephew of Queen Anne and reputed cross-dresser, serves as governor of New York and New Jersey until 1708.

1842 Tabloid newspaper *The Whip* goes on a rampage against the city's "sodomites," naming names from among what was clearly a somewhat developed community around City Hall.

1846 The newly created NYPD dismisses Edward McCosker for "indecently feeling the privates" of another man while on duty near City Hall; it was his second manhandling offense in as many months.

1849 Sensationalist novel *City Crimes* is printed, mentioning City Hall Park (map H1) as a center of male prostitution; meanwhile Herman Melville's *Redburn* is published, wherein a character remembers men "standing in sentimental attitudes" in front of nearby Palmo's Opera House (39–41 Chambers St., at Elk St., map H2).

LOWER MANHATTAN GAY TIMELINE

1939 In advance of the World's Fair, Mayor Fiorello LaGuardia orders a citywide shakedown of known gay and lesbian haunts.

1951 Chief City Magistrate John Murtagh announces a drive to subject "perverts" to more severe penalties.

1962 Public radio station WBAI broadcasts the groundbreaking *Live and Let Live,* featuring eight gay men in their 20s frankly discussing homosexuality; local media goes wild.

1978 Mayor Ed Koch prohibits sexual orientation discrimination within city government.

1986 A decade and a half after having been introduced, a bill barring sexual orientation discrimination is passed by the New York City Council.

1987 In response to what he sees as the political impotency of Gay Men's Health Crisis (which he had also cofounded), Larry Kramer founds ACT UP (AIDS Coalition To Unleash Power), which within weeks stages its first public action when 250 members block rush hour traffic on Wall Street at Broadway (map H3); 17 are arrested.

LOWER MANHATTAN, CHINATOWN, AND TRIBECA

LOWER MANHATTAN GAY TIMELINE

1990 Queer Nation is formed in protest of continued antigay prejudice, and as its first action members descend on straight bar Flutie's (Pier 17, South Street Seaport, map H4) to prove that queers will no longer restrict themselves and mutual displays of affection to gay-only establishments.

2001 At least 24 openly gay people die in the September 11 attacks, including New York Fire Department Catholic Chaplain Father Mychal Judge, killed while ministering to a fallen firefighter at the World Trade Center.

LODGING

RITZ-CARLTON BATTERY PARK With its incomparably breathtaking views of the Statue of Liberty, Ellis Island, and the downtown and Jersey skylines, the Ritz-Carlton Battery Park is an exquisite property offering luxury typical of the brand with the undeniable uniqueness of lying at the southernmost tip of Manhattan. Though it's a bit removed from Midtown and many of the city's top tourist attractions, it's perfect for Financial District business or anyone who doesn't mind a few pricey cab rides (or navigating the subways) to get uptown. Harbor view rooms even come with telescopes for sneaking close-up peeks at Lady Liberty. 2 West St. (between 1st Pl. and Battery Pl., map L1), 212-344-0800 or 800-241-3333, WWW.RITZCARLTON.COM/EN/PROPERTIES/ BATTERYPARK **EXPENSIVE**

ACTIVITIES

RIVER TO RIVER FESTIVAL This phenomenally popular and far-flung annual summer slate of free art events, begun as a downtown revitalization project post-9/11, has in past years seen concerts by Belle & Sebastian and the New Pornographers. RIVERTORIVER NYC.COM

STATEN ISLAND FERRY Great views of downtown Manhattan, plus free transport to Staten Island. What more can you ask of a boat? Twenty-five minutes each way. Whitehall Terminal, 1 Whitehall St. (at South St., map A2), NYC.GOV/HTML/DOT/HTML/FERRYBUS/STATFERY.SHTML

STATUE OF LIBERTY/ELLIS ISLAND IMMIGRATION MUSEUM Greeting tired poor huddled masses with a bright green American "howdy" since 1886, Lady Liberty's our kind of gal. A few things to bear in mind for your visit: You must reserve a Monument Pass in advance if you want to go inside the statue, you will need to go through two rounds of airport-type security (one at the ferry and one at the statue), and you cannot bring anything (backpack,

4

LOWER MANHATTAN, CHINATOWN, AND TRIBECA

OUT TRAVELER RATINGS GUIDE: MANHATTAN

GAY-FRIENDLY: ▼▼▼▼
GAY SCENE: ▼▼▼▼
LESBIAN SCENE: ▼▼▼
PRO-GAY LAWS: ▼▼▼
HIV RESOURCES: ▼▼▼▼

etc.) larger than a milk crate (apparently you may, however, bring as many ounces of shampoo as you like). On the trip back to Manhattan, ferries stop at Ellis Island; you don't have to get off and go into the Immigration Museum (ELLISISLAND.COM), but you'll be fascinated if you do. Ferries board at Battery Park, map A3, info 212-561-4588, STATUEOFLIBERTY.ORG or NPS.ORG/STLI, reservations 877-LADY-TIX or STATUECRUISES.COM

TRIBUTE WTC 9/11 VISITOR CENTER Visitors still feel powerfully drawn to the World Trade Center site, to pay respects and to try to make sense of what happened on that day in 2001. This very popular visitor center obliges, with walking tours and several powerful galleries of multimedia memories. Building on both the new Freedom Tower and the National September 11 Memorial and Museum is under way, but neither is scheduled for completion until 2011. Galleries $10, open M and W–Sa 10–6, Tu 12–6, Su 12–5. 120 Liberty St. (between Greenwich and Church Sts., map A4), 866-737-1184 or 212-393-9160 x138, TRIBUTENYC.ORG

DINING

BRIDGE CAFÉ In a structure dating from 1794 that in the 19th century housed a brothel, Bridge Café serves tasty new American cuisine from its lovely old American wood frame, in the shadow of the mighty Brooklyn Bridge. Strong on service and seafood, the buffalo steak is also a huge hit. 279 Water St. (between Dover St. and Peck Slip, map D1), 212-227-3344, EATGOODINNY.COM **MODERATE**

SHOPPING

CENTURY 21 No, not the real estate brokers—like you can afford property in downtown New York. You could be a bit richer though (or poorer, depending on how you look at it and how much you spend) after shopping at Century 21, New York's bargain basement for high-end fashion and home furnishings. This is where New Yorkers go to save. 22 Cortlandt St. (between Church St. and Broadway, map S1), 212-227-9092, C21STORES.COM

CHINATOWN

Except to get bigger, New York's Chinatown thankfully changes little through the march of time. In this dazzling world unto its own, you'll see, smell, and if you're daring even taste things that you're not likely to see, smell, or taste anywhere else this side of the

CHINATOWN GAY TIMELINE

1846 An editorial in working-class newspaper *The Subterranean* calls for local police to close down a "male brothel" on Bowery near Pell Street (map H5).

1876 *The Police Gazette* reports Billy McGlory's outrageous nightspot Armory Hall (156 Hester St., between Elizabeth and Mott Sts., map H6) to be home to "a number of simpering males who were painted to resemble women and togged up in feminine raiment, and who in falsetto voices exchanged disgusting badinage among themselves and with the patrons."

1908 Police charge a saloon run by Vito Lorenzo (207 Canal St., between Baxter and Mulberry Sts., map H7) with being "a fairy place."

4

IN THE STEPS OF PETER SEWALLY (A.K.A. MARY JONES, ETC.)

On June 11, 1836, New York City stone mason and white guy Robert Haslem went looking for a little nocturnal fun. He found it on Bleecker Street in the form of a pretty black prostitute, who took him to an alley near her house at **108 GREENE ST.** (between Prince and Spring Sts.), a known whorehouse, where they got down to business. Afterward they parted ways, only for Haslem to realize that his wallet was missing. He reported the event to police, who wasted no time in going undercover to catch the thieving hooker, and she was promptly nabbed. Or rather, he was promptly nabbed. Though the prostitute initially gave her name as Mary Jones, police realized during a strip search that she was genetically no she. Mary owned up to actually being Peter Sewally, cook and waiter by day, lady of the evening by night.

The local press of the era had a field day with the case. When it was revealed that Sewally had actually fashioned a makeshift vagina out of cow skin which he wore tied around his waist to fool/please his customers, he was dubbed Beefsteak Pete. The *New York Sun* reported that under the alternate monikers Miss Ophelia, Miss June, and Eliza Smith,

Yangtze. Chinese immigration to the area began in the mid-19th century and has continued apace ever since. Now home to the largest Chinese community in the Western Hemisphere, Chinatown NY has swallowed Little Italy nearly whole in recent decades, and has recently started noshing on the Lower East Side.

IN THE STEPS OF PETER SEWALLY (A.K.A. MARY JONES, ETC.)

Sewally "at night prowls about the **FIVE POINTS** (of *Gangs of New York* fame, near the modern corner of Baxter and Worth Sts., map P1) and other similar parts of the city, in the disguise of a female, for the purpose of enticing men into the dens of prostitution, where he picks their pockets if practicable."

At his trial a week post-capture, Sewally, who said he was 32 years old and a New York City native, denied ever meeting Haslem, much less taking his or any other wallet. He also seemed surprised that anyone would be shocked by his cross-dressing. "I have always attended parties among the people of my own color dressed in this way—and in New Orleans I always dressed in this way," he said. He was found guilty of grand larceny and sentenced to five years in state prison, but reappeared in news accounts several times in the ensuing years, invariably for the same thing, to which he appears to have been quite committed despite the consequences. On May 16, 1853, the *New York Times* reported that at 3 A M the previous morning, Sewally was arrested just days after being released from yet another five-year sentence at Sing Sing. It's the last we know of his whereabouts.

DINING

With so many incredible options about, it's said that the worst restaurant in New York's Chinatown would be the best Chinese in most any other city. Given that the home country comprises many distinct regions and styles, fare in the neighborhood can differ greatly from place to place, from Cantonese to Shanghaian to Szechuan and far beyond.

NEW GREEN BO Getting seated at one of New Green Bo's 10 tables can be tough during peak hours, and you'll be none too wowed by the décor while you wait. But then comes the Shanghai surprise: excellent food all around, with dumplings to die for. Extra happy special bonus: the fantastic Chinatown Ice Cream Factory is right across the street. 66 Bayard St. (between Mott and Elizabeth Sts., map D2), 212-625-2359.

SHOPPING

CANAL STREET A draw for locals and tourists alike, Canal Street between Bowery and Broadway (map S2) is jammed with shops and

CHINATOWN

stalls hawking everything from clothing to jewelry to electronics to movies and music, much of it of questionable quality and/or legality. But at these prices, who's complaining? Check out the fascinating fish and herb markets that are interspersed, too.

TRIBECA

The **TRI**angle **BE**low **CA**nal Street (running down to Chambers and east to Broadway) was a mostly overlooked industrial area until, starting in the '70s and gaining momentum in the '80s and '90s, artists and the wealthy began settling in the neighborhood's large former warehouse spaces. Today, some of the city's biggest celebrity residents live here, and it's become a de facto film industry hub.

ACTIVITY

TRIBECA FILM FESTIVAL Though it's only on from late April to early May, the Tribeca Film Festival has in the 20 years since its Robert DeNiro-helmed launch evolved into New York City's most important cinematic event. 212-941-2100, TRIBECAFILM FESTIVAL.ORG

LODGING

TRIBECA GRAND Perfect for the achingly hip wealthy rock star in you, the Tribeca Grand is a 203-room celeb and alterna-businessguy refuge offering easy access to SoHo, the Financial District, and of course trendy Tribeca itself. Some rooms (which tend toward the small but are packed with techy delights) overlook the hotel's oft-noisy Church Lounge atrium, but that's all part of the vibey allure. 2 Sixth Ave. (at White St., map L2), 212-519-6600, TRIBECAGRAND. COM **EXPENSIVE**

TRIBECA GRAND HOTEL

DINING

NOBU The restaurant that spawned a worldwide empire, chef Nobu Matsuhisa's namesake is still a hot ticket, serving South American-slanted Japanese fusion to the city's beautiful people. If reservations prove tough, try neighbor/sister Next Door Nobu, which is first-come first-served for some of the city's freshest sushi and finest Japanese fare. 105 Hudson St. (between Franklin and N. Moore Sts., map D3), 212-219-0500, MYRIADRESTAURANTGROUP.COM
EXPENSIVE

SHOPPING

STEVEN ALAN This flagship of Steven Alan's several New York clothing stores is the biggest and most diverse, carrying a cool coed blend of brands like A.P.C. and Nice Collective as well as (naturally) Alan's own line, and some nifty grooming supplies and housewares to boot. 103 Franklin St. (between Church St. and W. Broadway, map S3), 212-343-0692, STEVENALAN.COM

MEATPACKING

WEST VILLAGE

GREENWICH VILLAGE

SOHO

NOLITA

H19•
•S5
•H20
Little W 12th St
H18• L5•
•D6
•D4
Gansevoort St
Horatio St
Jane St
W 12th St
•H6
ACEL (Eighth Ave/14th St)
123 (14th St)
A2•
FLV (Sixth Ave/14th St)
•L3
L2• •N2
•H12
Bank St
W 11th St
S2•
•H11
Perry St
S1•
Charles St
•H10 H8•
(Christopher St)1
A3/N9 •S3
•N8 N7
•D4
P1• W 10th St
W 9th St
W 8th St
S4•
A1•
H15•
N4•
T1• •H14
•N3 L1• •N1 •N6
Grove St
D3•
Barrow St
D1•
L4•
ABCDEFV (W 4th St)
•N5
Morton St
•D5
H5•
Leroy St
D7• H16•
F5• H3•
•A4/H13
RW (NYU/8th St)
6 (Astor P
•H9
Clarkson St
•P2
P1• W 4th St/Wash Sq S
W 3rd St
•D2
•H2
(Houston St)1 •F4
•H1
S6• •H21
Charlton St
H17•
(Bleecker St)6
BDFV (Broadway/Lafayette)
(Spring St)CE
L6•
(Prince St)RW
•H22
•S9
S8•
D7•
6 (Spring St)
(Canal St)1
(Canal St)ACE
G4•
•G5
S7•
(Bowery)JMZ
(Canal St)NQRW

GREENWICH/WEST VILLAGE

First a word about naming conventions: Greenwich Village's boundaries are hotly debated, some claiming that they encompass the entire area between Houston and 14th Street from river to river, including the East Village. For others, Greenwich Village and West Village are two separate entities, the former being between Broadway to Sixth Avenue, and the latter between Sixth and the Hudson. For most though, Greenwich Village runs from Broadway westward and actually includes the West, which begins at Sixth Avenue. Got it? No worries, as it's really not that important for the visitor. Just call it the Village and you'll be fine.

If Lenape Indians weren't the first humans here, they were the ones the Dutch found when they settled this then-marshy area in 1629. The village that sprouted from that settlement was initially called Noordwijck, but by the early 1700s became Greenwich (historians are divided about whether it was via an Anglicization of Greenwijck or after the Greenwich in London). The village was a small, largely rural community that developed separately from Revolution-era New York City to the south. It wasn't until successive cholera and yellow fever epidemics hit New York in the early 1800s that city dwellers in search of cleaner air began settling here in large numbers, most notably during an outbreak in 1822.

By the early 1900s the Village had become an enclave of bohemianism, luring subsequent generations of artists, writers, poets, musicians, and dancers to settle here. The bohemian tradition flourished throughout the century as the Village became a center for beatniks in the '50s and folkies in the '60s. Gay culture simultaneously prospered, leading to the focused police harassment that in turn led to the Stonewall Riots that put the Village forever on the national map. Queers from across the country (and indeed, the world) flocked here in even greater numbers in the '70s.

By the late '80s, soaring rents began pushing the gay community northward into Chelsea, and it was largely replaced in the Village by those who could afford it, generally a more mainstream sort. Still, the neighborhood retains and is proud of its bohemian charm and history. It's also home to quite a few celebrities, including gay faves like Amy Sedaris and Sarah Jessica Parker. And no Greenwich Village discussion would be complete without mention of the ever-present and still ever-growing New York University, hubbed on the Village's east side but with a scurrying student populace that spills outward in all directions.

ACTIVITIES

In an area so steeped in gay history, it's only natural that the best things to do are decidedly gay-centric. Not that there's anything wrong with that.

CHRISTOPHER STREET PIER/HUDSON RIVER PARK Long a place where gays and lesbians of all colors, shapes, and sizes have congregated in freedom, Christopher Street Pier (or Pier 45, as it's officially called) was one of the first piers to be renovated as part of the city's massive Hudson River Park project, reopening in 2003. Now it's lusciously verdant and still a place for gays of all ilks—plus the entire Greenwich Village section (from Clarkson St. to Horatio St.) is the only area of Hudson River Park to provide free wireless Internet. Map A1, 212-627-2020, HUDSONRIVERPARK.ORG/ PARKMAP/GVAREA.HTM

THE LESBIAN, GAY, BISEXUAL & TRANSGENDER COMMUNITY CENTER Hanging out at the local gay and lesbian center might not seem very exciting, but that's because you've never been to The Center. So tapped into so many facets of New York City gay life is The Center that each week more than 300 groups meet here, and 6,000 people pass through its doors. No two visits to The Center are the same, as you ride the elevator with bingo-playing lesbians one time and cowboy speed daters the next. 208 W. 13th St. (at Seventh Ave., map A2), 212-620-7310, GAYCENTER.ORG

STONEWALL INN Recently renovated and reopened under new ownership, the Stonewall Inn is, of course, the site of the riots during which our last gay nerve got sparked into the revolution that changed everything. It's now a National Historic Monument. 53 Christopher St. (between W. 4th St. and Waverly Pl., map A3), STONEWALL-PLACE.COM

WASHINGTON SQUARE PARK Set at the picturesque heart of the greater East/West Village area, Washington Square Park has a colorful counterculture history, offering respite through the eras to beatniks, hippies, breakdancers, skatepunks, and the ever-present NYUers. Between W. 4th St. and Waverly Pl., at the foot of Fifth Ave (map A4).

GREENWICH/WEST VILLAGE GAY TIMELINE

1890 Republican Party newspaper the *New York Press* prints article "The Wickedest Place" in New York about The Slide (157 Bleecker St., between Thompson and Sullivan Sts., map H1), which it claims is nightly full of males "not worthy the name of man. They are effeminate, degraded and addicted to vices which are inhuman and unnatural."

1892 "It is a fact," reports the *New York Herald,* "that The Slide and the unspeakable nature of the orgies practised there are a matter of common talk among men who are bent on taking in the town, making a night of it"; the place is promptly closed.

1894 In the book *The Doctor and the Devil, or the Midnight Adventures of Dr. Parkhurst,* author Charles Gardner relays Parkhurst's experience at male brothel the Golden Rule Pleasure Club (W. Third St.): "In each room sat a youth, whose face was painted, eye-brows blackened, and whose airs were those of a young girl. Each person talked in a high falsetto voice, and called the others by women's names."

1899 While intended to be rooting out municipal waste and inefficiency, the Mazet Committee reports on "male degenerate" hangouts the Black Rabbit (183 Bleecker

St., between MacDougal and Sullivan Sts.) and the Artistic Club (13th St., between Fifth and Sixth Aves., map H2).

1912 Feminist luncheon club Heterodoxy is formed "for unorthodox women" including prominent lesbian members Sara Josephine Baker and partners Katharine Anthony and Elisabeth Irwin; they often meet at Polly's Restaurant (137 MacDougal St., between 3rd and 4th Sts., map H3).

1925 Police descend on a slew of known gay-frequented establishments in Greenwich Village, leaving just three open.

1925 Polish Jewish immigrant Eve Kotchever (who goes by the name Eve Addams) opens Eve's Hangout (129 MacDougal St. at W. Third St., map H4), a lesbian tea room and speakeasy with a sign on its door proclaiming "Men are admitted but not welcome"; the following year she's raided by police and sent to a workhouse for a year before being deported for writing a collection of short stories called *Lesbian Love.*

1948 Jack Lait and Lee Mortimer's book *New York: Confidential!,* an exposé of "The Big City After Dark,"

GREENWICH/WEST VILLAGE
GAY TIMELINE

says "not all New York's queer (or, as they say it, 'gay') people live in Greenwich Village."

1950 Beats-to-be Allen Ginsberg and Gregory Corso meet at the lesbian Pony Stable Inn (150 W. 4th St. at Sixth Ave., map H5).

1950 The Sea Colony (52 Eighth Ave., between Horatio and W. 4th Sts., map H6), though subject to constant police harassment, is one of the most popular lesbian bars.

1958 Caffe Cino (31 Cornelia St., between Bleecker and W. 4th Sts., map H7) opens, serving a largely gay and bohemian clientele and spawning the development of off-Broadway theater.

1966 To protest a State Liquor Authority policy denying gay people the right to be served at bars, Mattachine Society members stage a "sip-in" at the still-open Julius (159 W. 10th St., at Waverly Pl., map H8), which Rudolph Nureyev, Truman Capote, and Tennessee Williams are also said to have frequented over the years.

1967 The Oscar Wilde Bookshop (original location 291 Mercer St., at Waverly St., map H9) opens, becoming the first gay bookstore in the country.

GREENWICH/WEST VILLAGE GAY TIMELINE

1968 Oscar Wilde owner Craig Rodwell begins editing the *New York HYMNAL,* written exclusively for the gay community and spreading such slogans as "Gay Power" and "Gay Is Good."

1969 Despite a several-year decline in gay bar raids, police descend on the Stonewall Inn (51 Christopher St., between W. 4th St. and Waverly Pl.) on June 28, sparking a violent riot during which more than 2,000 protesters confronted over 400 police.

1969 Around 500 people march down a heavily policed Christopher Street on July 2 in the first Gay Pride demonstration.

1969 The first Gay Power group convenes in Greenwich Village on July 9, producing the manifesto *What Homosexuals Want*.

1970 After-hours gay bar The Snake Pit (211 W. 10th St., at Bleecker St., map H10) is raided on March 8 and everyone present is arrested, including Argentine national Diego Vinales, who is so distraught that he jumps from the second floor precinct window (135 Charles St., between Greenwich and Washington Sts.), only to be impaled on six 14-inch spikes on a fence

GREENWICH/WEST VILLAGE GAY TIMELINE

below; he lives, but only barely, becoming a rallying figure of the new activist movement through slogans like "Any way you look at it, that boy was pushed!"

1970 Thousands walk from Washington Place and Sixth Avenue to Sheep Meadow in Central Park in the first Christopher Street Gay Liberation Day March on June 28, the first anniversary of the Stonewall Riots.

1971 The first act of Harvey Fierstein's *Torch Song Trilogy* is set during this year at gay bar International Stud (733 Greenwich St. at Perry St., map H11).

1972 The Gay Switchboard is launched at the newly opened Liberation House (247 11th St., between 4th St. and Waverly Pl., map H12) and begins logging 400 calls a week.

1973 Ex-nun and future LGBT leader Jean O'Leary makes her public debut on the Washington Square Park stage (map H13) of the annual Gay Pride rally and declares transvestite entertainment insulting to women; the bedlam that ensues between girl homos and boy homos can only be placated by Bette Midler's rousing rendition of "Friends."

GREENWICH/WEST VILLAGE GAY TIMELINE

1980 Popular late '70s/early '80s lesbian hangout Duchess (101 Seventh Ave. South at Grove St., map H14) begins coming under attack from state liquor license inspectors who are reportedly refused service after charming bartenders with refrains of "Come on girlie, give us a drink."

1980 Former city transit cop Ronald Crumpley goes on a shooting rampage in the Village, killing two and wounding six in front of The Ramrod (394 West St., between 10th and Christopher Sts., map H15). "I want to kill them all," he explains afterward. "They're no good. They ruin everything." He is found not guilty of murder by reason of insanity.

1981 Eighty men meet at writer Larry Kramer's Washington Square North apartment to address the "rare cancer seen in 41 homosexuals" (as reported by the *New York Times*) and to raise research funds; the gathering would lay the foundation for the Gay Men's Health Crisis.

1985 The Harvey Milk School opens with 20 gay teenage students at the Washington Square United Methodist Church (135 W. 4th St., between MacDougal St. and Sixth Ave., map H16).

GREENWICH/WEST VILLAGE GAY TIMELINE

1992 George Segal's controversial statue "Gay Liberation" is installed in Christopher Park across from the Stonewall.

2007 In a rather shockingly under-the-gaydar event harkening back to targeted raids of decades past, police descend on trendy gay hotspot Mr. Black (643 Broadway at Bleecker St., map H17) over Labor Day weekend, and not only are 15 patrons arrested for suspicion of drug use, but 17 staff members as well— on the dubious grounds of "criminal nuisance" for having ignored what was going on around them; all but three are released without being charged.

LODGING

Since relatively little of the Greenwich/West Village area has been torn down and replaced with larger buildings over the years, much of its accommodation comes in the form of smallish guest houses. While these properties offer a lovely and infinitely homier experience, they also generally have far more stringent rules than large hotels. Minimum stays can run up to five nights, and having anyone but a registered guest in your room can be a big no-no. Those wanting more flexibility should steer toward the Washington Square Hotel or the Gansevoort just to the Village's north.

ABINGDON GUEST HOUSE Spread across two landmarked 1850s Federal-style townhouses, the Abingdon offers nine brightly (but very tastefully) paletted and well-appointed rooms, each with its own bath. A handy online tool allows you to view both the décor and availability of each of the nine rooms, but also repeatedly warns that they expect mature, quiet guests only. As long as you don't mind admitting that you're now mature and quiet, it's a definite score among properties in its price class. 13 and 21 Eighth Ave. (between Jane and 12th Sts., map L2), 212-243-5384, ABINGDONGUESTHOUSE.COM **MODERATE**

GREENWICH VILLAGE HABITUÉ Such a little known secret that we can't even give out its exact address, the Greenwich Village Habitué receives little but gushing praise from those lucky enough to have already discovered it. Matthew and Kevin, the onsite-living hosts in this 1830s Federal brownstone, have long been in the business of fine arts and antiques, and it shows in the wonderful room appointments. The property does have a five night minimum and doesn't take credit cards, but you won't find taste and hospitality like this at a similar price anywhere else in the entire city. Christopher St. (between Greenwich and Hudson Sts., map L1), 212-243-6495, GVHABITUE.COM **MODERATE**

INCENTRA VILLAGE HOUSE Offering many of the same charming assets as the Abingdon across the street, the Incentra Village House has 12 studio rooms (all with private bath, some with kitchenette and/or fireplace) and one extremely well-valued suite. The garden room is also a steal, with sole access to the property's private garden. 32 Eighth Ave. (between Jane and 12th Sts., map L3), 212-206-0007, INCENTRAVILLAGE.COM **MODERATE**

IN THE STEPS OF MURRAY HALL

Understanding Murray Hall takes a quick lesson in the now foreign world of New York City's Tammany Hall politics, made famous in the movie *Gangs of New York* and an important local fixture for nearly two centuries. To nutshell it, Tammany held a firm grasp on the city's Democratic political machinery, largely by virtue of its control on the city's immigrant populace, who, disenfranchised from other government institutions, embraced Tammany's indulgences like apartment finding and job placement. In turn, Tammany expected their votes come election time.

Enter into this framework Murray Hall, a Scotland-born bloke who around 1875 opened an employment agency on 23rd Street and Sixth Avenue. By the mid-1880s he and his second wife had moved to **145 SIXTH AVENUE** (between 10th and 11th Streets, map P1; Sixth Avenue was renumbered in the 1920s), where the likeable Hall soon became one of the area's most popular "politicians"—a term that in those days included anyone involved in shaping the Tammany voting bloc, which Hall, as an employment placer and bondsman serving mostly immigrants, clearly was. "Politics" of the era also required a fair

WASHINGTON SQUARE HOTEL With its killer address overlooking Washington Square Park and set smack between the East and West Villages, the Washington Square Hotel is an excellent option for the downtown-centric visitor, offering straightforwardly simple, clean, and wallet-friendly rooms. 103 Waverly Pl. (at Washington Square North, map L4), 800-222-0418, WSHOTEL.COM **MODERATE**

IN THE STEPS OF MURRAY HALL

amount of drinking with one's fellow Tammany buddies, at which by all accounts Hall was quite adept.

When Hall died in 1901, virtually everyone who knew him was shocked to learn that he was actually genetically a woman who had been born Mary Anderson. "A woman?" exclaimed Joseph Young, lieutenant of a local New York state senator. "Why, he'd line up at the bar and take his whiskey like any veteran, and didn't make faces over it, either. If he was a woman he ought to have been born a man, for he lived and looked like one."

Tragically, Hall had been suffering from breast cancer for several years, and had attempted self-treatment until the very end for fear of being exposed. His doctor later reported that the cancer had eaten away almost to the heart. Hall's wife had died three years earlier, but they left behind an adopted daughter, Minnie (Millie on the 1900 census, where she's listed as age 20, and Murray 60). Hall was buried in Queens's Mount Olivet Cemetery, according to a *New York Times* account dressed in women's clothing for the first time in 30 years.

DINING

BABBO The flagship of Mario Batali's ever-growing eatery empire, Babbo has been pleasing palates for a decade now with the chef's uniquely inventive Italian menu (beef cheek ravioli with crushed squab liver and black truffles…just like Mom used to make!). A true bonus is the restaurant itself: casual, lively, and friendly, none of which you'd expect to find at a place of this caliber. The only down side is trying to get a reservation, even after all these years: *Time Out New York* gave it the 2007 Eat Out Award for Best Restaurant You Can't Get Into. 110 Waverly Pl. (between McDougall St. and Sixth Ave., map D1), 212-777-0303, BABBONYC.COM **EXPENSIVE**

MAS (FARMHOUSE) Perfect for a romantic dinner or anyone seeking fantastic French food served amidst a bit of modern swank, Mas (farmhouse) [that's the full name, lest you not be familiar enough with southern French Catalan to know that *mas* means "farmhouse" serves seasonal fare done creatively but simply, and

WASHINGTON SQUARE PARK

the result is simply divine. As an added plus, they're open until 4 AM, serving from a late night menu after 11:30. 39 Downing St. (at Bedford St., map D2), 212-255-1790, MASFARMHOUSE.COM **EXPENSIVE**

THE LITTLE OWL With a delectable Mediterranean/new American menu, a prime West Village location (with windows showcasing all its surrounding glory), and a staff that everyone agrees is just plain "nice," The Little Owl is a true gem. Only problem is that with some great word of mouth but seating for just around 30, the place fills quickly, so book well ahead. If you get in, start with the gravy meatball sliders. 90 Bedford St. (at Grove St., map D3), 212-741-4695, THELITTLEOWLNYC.COM **MODERATE**

FLORENT For over 20 years, Restaurant Florent has served as a priceless slice of what's great about New York City: extremely diverse humanity coming together in total harmony. Maybe it's the excellent French-leaning comfort food. Maybe it's the shockingly cheap prices. Maybe it's the cool vibe instilled by owner and neighborhood champion Florent Morellet. Whatever it is, it works, and it does so 24 hours a day. 69 Gansevoort St. (between Greenwich and Washington Sts., map D4), 212-989-5779, RESTAURANTFLORENT.COM **MODERATE**

JOHN'S OF BLEECKER STREET Ask a hundred New Yorkers where to get the best slice of pizza and you're liable to get 90 different answers, but at least 10 votes will surely go to John's, the brick-ovened West Village fave through the years of the likes of Frank Sinatra and Al Pacino. 278 Bleecker St. (between Sixth and Seventh Aves., map D5), 212-243-1680, JOHNSOFBLEECKERSTREET.COM **INEXPENSIVE**

SHOPPING

MARC BY MARC JACOBS MENSWEAR Expanding his takeover of Bleecker Street, Marc Jacobs opened this heavenly hip "Marc by" menswear shop here in 2007, and choirs of moneyed bohemian angels have been singing ever since. 382 Bleecker St. (at Perry St., map S1), 212-929-0304, MARCJACOBS.COM

MAGNOLIA BAKERY Magnolia's mid-'90s opening spawned the "cupcake craze," and hollas along the way from such beloved gay heavyweights as *Sex and the City* and *The Devil Wears Prada* haven't hurt. Open late, so stuff yourself silly between dinner and drinks. 401 Bleecker St. (at W. 11th St., map S2), 212-462-2572, MAGNOLIACUPCAKES.COM

OSCAR WILDE BOOKSHOP The world's oldest gay and lesbian book emporium, Oscar Wilde Bookshop has lovingly colored rainbow reading lists for over 40 years. 15 Christopher St. (at Gay St., map S3), 212-255-8097, OSCARWILDEBOOKS.COM

STRAND BOOKSTORE An 80-year-old city institution, the Strand was once one of 48 bookstores that formed Book Row and lined Broadway from Astor Place to Union Square. Today it's a glorious holdout from pre-megachain days, with "18 miles" of books—mostly gently used, but new ones, too, plus the city's largest selection of rare editions. 828 Broadway (at 12th St., map S4), 212-473-1452, STRANDBOOKS.COM

NIGHTLIFE

West Village gay nightlife has unabashedly and thankfully resisted the pull of passing trends for decades now, making going out here often feel like a surreal but refreshing step back in time.

CHI CHIZ Amiable spot with a predominantly black crowd. 135 Christopher St. (between Hudson and Greenwich Sts., map N1), 212-462-0027

THE CUBBY HOLE Picked by *New York* magazine as the city's Best Lesbian Bar of 2007, The Cubby Hole is for real girls, but is usually very mixed. 281 W 12th St. (between W. 4th and Greenwich Sts., map N2), 212-243-9041, CUBBYHOLEBAR.COM

THE DUGOUT Friendly bear den. The Dugout is where the manly meet in the Village. 185 Christopher St. (at Weehawken St., map N3), 212-242-9113, THEDUGOUTNY.COM

THE HANGAR A straightforwardly hunky, cruisey, attitude-free gay bar. 115 Christopher St. (between Hudson and Bleecker Sts., map N4), 212-627-2044, MYSPACE.COM/HANGARNYC

HENRIETTA HUDSON Mostly for the ladies, the hot Henrietta Hudson is welcoming of male-persuasioned gays too. 438 Hudson St. (at Morton St., map N5), 212-924-3347, HENRIETTA HUDSON.COM

MARIE'S CRISIS This singing saloon may be where old musical theater students go to die, but it's also a hard-to-resist rollicking good time for anyone, and the mix of the crowd—all smiling, most singing—proves it. 59 Grove St. (between Bleecker St. and Seventh Ave. South, map N6), 212-243-9323

THE MONSTER The Monster rocks it 2-for-1 old school with a piano bar upstairs and disco down. 80 Grove St. (at Sheridan Square, map N7), 212-924-3558, MANHATTAN-MONSTER.COM

GREENWICH / WEST VILLAGE, MEATPACKING DISTRICT, AND SOHO / NOLITA

5

PIECES Friendly Pieces delightfully harkens back to your first gay bar, rainbows and all. 8 Christopher St. (between Gay St. and Greenwich Ave., map N8), 212-929-9291, PIECESBAR.COM

THE STONEWALL INN This site where the gay revolution began is now renovated and reopened yet again under new management. 53 Christopher St. (between W. 4th St. and Waverly Pl., map N9), 212-488-2705, THESTONEWALLINN.NET

MEATPACKING DISTRICT

Once home to, well, actual meat packers, and later to the scandalous sex trucks seen in the documentary *Gay Sex in the 70s* (lending a second *entendre* to the Meatpacking name), this little neighborhood sandwiched between the West Village and Chelsea has been completely revitalized over the last decade or so, now boasting some of the city's hippest boutiques, eateries, and nightspots. Watch for its further ascension when much-talked-about High Line park opens at Gansevoort Street this year.

LODGING

HOTEL GANSEVOORT Perhaps the L.A.-est of New York hotels, the Gansevoort has become somewhat of a nerve center for the ultratrendy District de Meatpacking. Its 187 rooms are naturally tastefully appointed and actually large by New York standards. The sumptuous rooftop pool (with underwater music) is a major attraction, drawing a closeup-ready mix of fashionistas, celebrities, and those who like to be near them. The gorgeous skyline views are also nice. 18 Ninth Ave. (at 13th St., map L5), 212-206-6700 or 877-426-7386, HOTELGANSEVOORT.COM **EXPENSIVE**

MEATPACKING DISTRICT GAY TIMELINE

1963 The State Liquor Authority revokes the licenses of often-raided gay hangouts including The Fawn (835 Washington St. at Little West 12th St., map H18).

1975 Disco king Jacques Morali spots Felipe Rose dancing in an Indian costume at wild gay club The Anvil (500 W. 14th St. at Tenth Ave., map H19), and the Village People are born.

1985 Amid growing HIV fears, gay sex club The Mineshaft (835 Washington St. at Little West 12th St., map H18) is shut down after nine years and nine days of existence, notably at the same location where The Fawn had been shut down 22 years earlier.

1991 Club impresarios Johnny Dynell and Chi Chi Valenti move the notoriously unique Jackie 60 from Nell's to its new address, which will later become Mother (432 W. 14th St. at Washington St., map H20) when the pair buy the space in 1996.

2000 *Sex and the City*'s Samantha Jones moves from the Upper East Side to 300 Gansevoort St. (a fictitious address, but one clearly meant to highlight the District's rising hipness).

DINING

PASTIS One of Keith McNally's many popular NYC creations, French brasserie Pastis, long known as a celeb and fashionista fave, has for some time now been *the* place to brunch and people-watch in Meatpacking. 9 Ninth Ave. (at Little W. 12th St., map D6), 212-929-4844 **MODERATE**

SHOPPING

New York retail home to such fashion-world giants as Alexander McQueen, Stella McCartney, Diane Von Furstenberg, and Carlos Miele, little Meatpacking packs one of the city's strongest high-end shopping punches.

JEFFREY There's dissension among New York's high fashion set about who's better at providing the hippest array of pricey designer duds, Barneys or Jeffrey; the consensus is generally that Barneys is bigger, but shopping at Jeffrey makes a stronger statement. 449 W. 14th St. (between Ninth and Tenth Aves., map S5), 212-206-1272, JEFFREYNEWYORK.COM

SOHO/NOLITA

Few places in Manhattan showcase how rapidly shape shifting the city can be as does SoHo. Less than 50 years ago virtually the entire neighborhood was an abandoned industrial zone, characterized as an enormous commercial slum in a City Club of New York report. As part of the Robert Moses–championed Lower Manhattan Expressway plan (which would've connected the Holland Tunnel to the Manhattan and Williamsburg Bridges), much of the area was scheduled to be decimated. Fortunately local artists, who'd already (albeit illegally) begun to move into

SOHO/NOLITA GAY TIMELINE

1977 Revolutionary multiracial straight-friendly gay club Paradise Garage (84 King St., between Varick and Hudson Sts., map H21) opens.

1992 MTV's *The Real World* debuts, with a New York City loft (565 Broadway at Prince, #2C, map H22) as its first backdrop and Norm Korpi as its first gay housemate.

2005 Singer, songwriter, and DJ Boy George calls police to his Nolita apartment (Centre St.) to report that he's been nearly burgled by a hustler; cops find 13 bags of cocaine, which George claims were planted by the prostitute, but he is arrested all the same and sentenced to community service.

the hulking cast iron skeletons, banded together to fight the expressway project. By the late 1960s the growing arts community had been dubbed SoHo, by virtue of its southern (So) location relative to Houston Street (Ho).

SoHo reigned supreme as the city's art gallery capital through the '70s and '80s, until a mass exodus saw them flee to the lower rents of Chelsea in the '90s. Since then SoHo has become more or less a glorified (and very pricey) massive open-air shopping mall, albeit with far trendier tenants than you'll find at your average buyplex. On weekends the streets can be more crowded here than anywhere else in the city, with tourists and locals alike scurrying from one hip merchant to the next.

Especially in the last decade, SoHo's style has crept westward into what was formerly just the northern section of Little Italy, but has since been rechristened with the trendier-sounding Nolita (North of Little ITAly). This stretch between Broadway and Bowery is home to some of downtown's hippest boutiques.

ACTIVITIES

SEE IN ART: Deitch Projects, Leslie/Lohman Gallery

LODGING

HOTEL (THE MERCER) Oozing as much cool as it did when it burst onto the scene a decade ago, Hotel (The Mercer) is still the only downtown choice for a host of celebs and other bicoastal moneyed gadabouts (this is where Russell Crowe famously hurled a phone at an unwitting concierge in 2005; Calvin Klein lives here, too). The views are amazing, and its location is perfect for SoHo shopping sprees and quick access to the nearby West Village. 147 Mercer St. (at Prince St., map L6), 212-966-6060, MERCERHOTEL. COM **EXPENSIVE**

DINING

BALTHAZAR Widely hailed as the best French brasserie outside of Paris, Keith McNally's Balthazar is truly a gem, serving the rich, the famous, and the rest of us with the same lively panache. Perfect for loading up on carbs and prestige for a Sunday shopping stroll through SoHo and Nolita. Call as far in advance as possible, especially for coveted weekend reservations. 80 Spring St. (between Broadway and Crosby St., map D7), 212-965-1414, BALTHAZARNY.COM **EXPENSIVE**

SHOPPING

JACQUES TORRES CHOCOLATE It's the closest you'll ever come to Wonkaland, and no pesky golden tickets required. In this 8,000 square foot west SoHo choco-paradise, watch the god-food being made from start to finish, then ingest away at the onsite café. 350 Hudson St. (at King St., map S6), 212-414-2462, MRCHOCOLATE.COM

MUJI Gays and young girls alike went crazy when this, the first dedicated U.S. outlet of Japanese minimalist paper-product sensation Muji opened its doors in late 2007. 455 Broadway (between Grand and Howard Sts., map S7), 212-334-2002, MUJI.COM

SEIZE SUR VINGT Suits with style dress up at Seize Sur Vingt, with its perfectly posh and sublimely rendered array of white-collar workwear. 243 Elizabeth St. (between Houston and Prince Sts., map S8), 212-343-0476, 16SUR20.COM

UNIQLO Also unique to New York for now is Uniqlo, the Japanese bargain trendsetter whose slick SoHo outlet is the growing chain's global flagship. 546 Broadway, (between Prince and Spring Sts., map S9), 917-237-8800, UNIQLO.COM

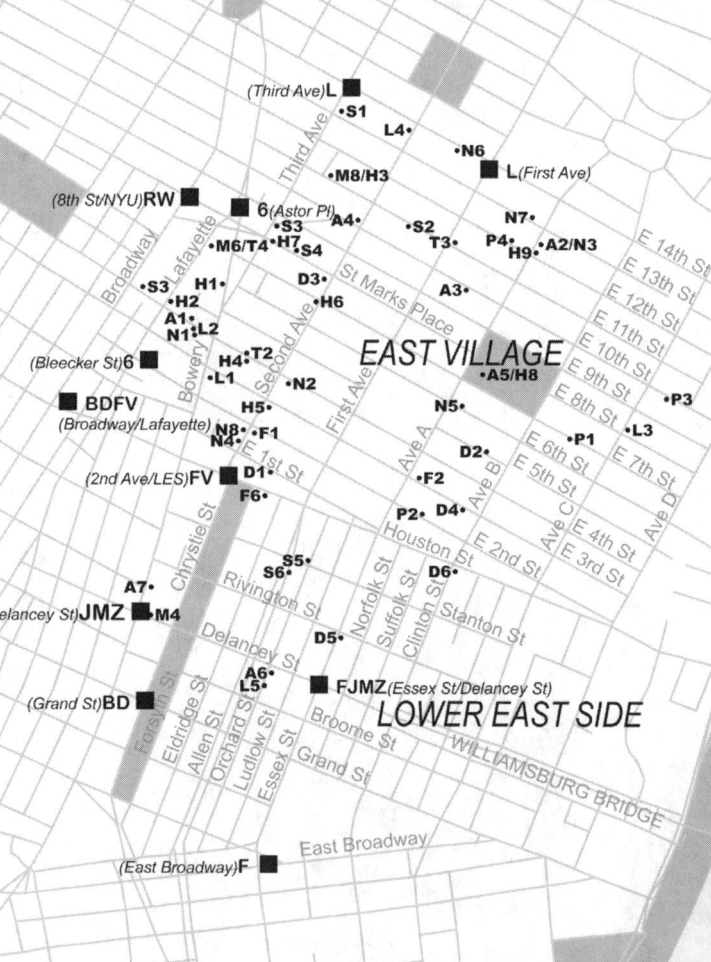

EAST VILLAGE

LOWER EAST SIDE

(Third Ave)L
(8th St/NYU)RW
6(Astor Pl)
(Bleecker St)6
BDFV
(Broadway/Lafayette)
(2nd Ave/LES)FV
JMZ(Delancey St)
(Grand St)BD
FJMZ(Essex St/Delancey St)
(East Broadway)F
L(First Ave)

Third Ave
Broadway
Lafayette
Bowery
Second Ave
First Ave
St Marks Place
Ave A
Ave B
Ave C
Ave D
Chrystie St
Forsyth St
Eldridge St
Allen St
Orchard St
Ludlow St
Essex St
Rivington St
Delancey St
Norfolk St
Suffolk St
Clinton St
Stanton St
Houston St
Broome St
Grand St
East Broadway
WILLIAMSBURG BRIDGE
E 1st St
E 2nd St
E 3rd St
E 4th St
E 5th St
E 6th St
E 7th St
E 8th St
E 9th St
E 10th St
E 11th St
E 12th St
E 13th St
E 14th St

S1 L4 N6 M8/H3 S3 A4 S2 T3 N7 P4 H9 A2/N3 M6/T4 H7 S4 M8 H1 H2 D3 H6 A3 S3 A1 N1 L2 T2 A5/H8 H4 L1 N2 N5 P3 H5 P1 L3 N8 F1 D2 N4 F2 P2 D4 F6 D1 S5 S6 D6 A7 M4 D5 A6 L5

EAST VILLAGE

Until the 1960s, there was no East Village, at least not in name. The area above Houston and east of Broadway (some say Bowery) was simply known as the northern part of the Lower East Side—that is, until enterprising developers saw a way to connect it tag-wise to the far more prosperous Greenwich Village.

At one time almost completely part of Peter Stuyvesant's 17th century *bouwerij,* or farm, the area later became the destination for several immigrant communities, including Germans, Ukrainians, Poles, Jews, Irish, Italians, and Puerto Ricans. In the '50s came the beatniks, including Jack Kerouac, Allen Ginsberg (see sidebar), and a host of other artists, writers, and musicians who embraced their gritty environs and gave the area even more countercultural cachet than Greenwich Village to the west.

Crime in the East Village escalated in the '70s and pushed out all but the heartiest, making way for the next wave of punks and new wavers who would reclaim the neighborhood in the '70s and early '80s. The area was largely a stark urban frontier in those days, with squatters taking up residence in the abandoned buildings that dotted the landscape, especially in the sub-hood of letter-named avenues to the east known as Alphabet City. These were formative years in the neighborhood's decidedly alternative modern gay scene as well, with creative collectives like Pyramid Club paving the way.

Left-leaning locals have been bemoaning the encroachment of gentrification ever since (local music landmark CBGB was finally forced to close in 2006, and at last report was slated to become a John Varvatos clothing store), but the area's managed to retain a combination of multicultural neighborhoodiness and hip edginess unlike any other sector of the city. Still, there's little denying that the massive high-profile construction boom currently under way, particularly along Bowery and Bond Streets, will be strongly impacting the changing face of the East Village in the coming years.

ACTIVITIES

The East Village is chockablock with such random character that simply walking around and local-color soaking is one of the neighborhood's best pastimes. Here are a few don't-miss spots to hit along the way.

MERCHANT'S HOUSE Step back in time at this, the city's oldest preserved family home. Built in 1832 by prosperous merchant Seabury Tredwell, the brick and marble row house remained in the family for the next century. Now it's on display for all with the family's original furnishings intact, a living showcase of a long bygone era amid the progress steaming ahead all around it. $8, open 12–5 Th–M. 29 E. 4th St. (between Bowery and Lafayette St., map A1), 212-777-1089, MERCHANTSHOUSE.COM

RAPTURE CAFÉ & BOOKS A fairly recent but extremely welcome addition to the East Village, this café/performance space/bookstore has become the nabe's alt-queer central, offering a daily slate of everything from bingo to comedy to Readings for Filth (the late Dean Johnson's creation). 200 Ave. A (between 12th and 13th Sts., map A2), 212-228-1177, RAPTURECAFE.COM

RUSSIAN AND TURKISH BATHS NOT a gay bathhouse (those have been gone from the East Village for some time), the Russian and Turkish Baths is the last of its kind in the neighborhood, having opened back in 1892 when its patrons were mostly local immigrants. These days, bathers range from celebs (like Leonardo DiCaprio and Uma Thurman) to hipsters to the nice Polish lady down the block. Take a scathingly hot Russian sauna or swelter in the Turkish or Swedish steam rooms, then go for a dip in the ice cold pool. Massages are also available (including Russian oak-broom *platzka* for the daring), and no appointments necessary (oh, and no happy endings either). Coed except for Wednesday mornings (for the ladies) and Sunday mornings (guys only). 268 E. 10th St. (between First Ave. and Ave. A, map A3), 212-473-8806, RUSSIANTURKISHBATHS.COM

ST. MARK'S CHURCH-IN-THE-BOWERY Built on the site of Peter Stuyvesant's former family chapel, St. Mark's has been an Episcopal church since 1799, now standing proudly and majestically askew from the grid-lined newer structures around it. During the church's long and ongoing history of arts friendliness, Isadora Duncan danced here in 1922, and Sam Shepard presented his first plays here in 1964. And you've gotta love a church that holds an annual Disco Mass in conjunction with Gay Pride. 10th St. and Second Ave. (NW corner, map A4), 212-674-6377, STMARKSCHURCH-IN-THE-BOWERY.COM

TOMPKINS SQUARE PARK Nearly from its inception in the mid-19th century, Tompkins Square Park was a site of protest. First it was the local immigrant populace decrying economic conditions. Later came anti-Vietnam protesters in the 1960s, then antigentrification championers in the '80s. The city closed the park for a year's renovation (and homeless-shooing) in the early '90s, and ever since Tompkins has been a mostly civilized square—though it still serves as home every September to the alternative Howl! Festival of East Village Arts (now sometimes encompassing Lady Bunny's notorious dragstravanganza Wigstock, which got its own start here in 1985). 7th to 10th Sts. (between Aves. A and B, map A5).

SEE LISTING IN FILM: Anthology Film Archives, Two Boots Pioneer Theater

SEE ALSO IN MUSIC: Joe's Pub, Webster Hall

SEE ALSO IN THEATER: New York Theatre Workshop, P.S. 122, Public Theater

LODGING

Despite the outcry from locals who don't want to see the East Village go the way of the ultratrendy (and ultrabusy into late night) Meatpacking District, fancy boutique hotels seem to be sprouting up in the area like so many shiny weeds. Next up by the end of '08 is the 23-story Cooper Square Hotel, which has already been dubbed "Dubai on the Bowery" for its resemblance to that country's soulless boom buildings.

THE BOWERY Arguably the hippest NYC hotel of the moment, this latest big venture from Maritime owners Sean MacPherson and Eric Goode opened in 2007, and seems to have ushered in a hotel building craze to the area. With its fast up-and-coming NoHo location, its unobstructed floor to ceiling views from all sides, and a lobby bar that's one of the city's most happening, the Bowery's got a lot to offer. Just mind your wallet on the way in, as it's currently flanked by a halfway house and a methadone clinic. 335 Bowery (at 3rd St., map L1), 212-505-9100, THEBOWERYHOTEL.COM **EXPENSIVE**

LAFAYETTE HOUSE The aforementioned MacPherson and Goode have quietly expanded their burgeoning local empire with the opening of this small (15 rooms) and understatedly elegant-cum-hip hotel just a block away from their Bowery property, and right next door to B Bar, which Goode also owns (and which hosts long-running Tuesday gay club-must Beige). The rooms at Lafayette House are richly appointed, and all have working fireplaces—plus *double* double-paned windows to insulate from any pesky street noise below. 38 East 4th St. (between Bowery and Lafayette St., map L2), 212-505-8100, LAFAYETTENYC.COM **EXPENSIVE**

EAST VILLAGE BED & COFFEE Coyly calling itself "a B&B without the breakfast," East Village Bed & Coffee is quite possibly the best sleep bargain in town (which indeed, the *New York Post* recently agreed). It's tucked a bit far down and east for some tastes and the baths are all shared, but for those wanting a clean and very pleasant explore-the-East Village address, this one's hard to match. Book far ahead. 110 Ave. C (between 7th and 8th Sts., map L3), 212-533-4175 or 917-816-0071, BEDANDCOFFEE.COM **INEXPENSIVE**

SECOND HOME ON SECOND AVENUE Fittingly owned by the former property's former partner, Second Home on Second Avenue is another incredible bargain that fills up fast. Here two of the seven rooms have private baths, and the location, just three blocks from Union Square, is phenomenal. 221 Second Ave. (between 13th and 14th Sts., map L4), 212-677-3161, SECONDHOMESECOND AVENUE.COM **INEXPENSIVE**

DINING

The East Village's hearty stew of cultures helps make it one of the city's best restaurant nabes, with scores of excellent choices for every taste bud and income bracket. Veselka at the corner of 9th St. and Second Ave. is great for demi-modernized Ukrainian fare, and don't miss famed Indian Row, where so many similar Indian restaurants crowd 6th Street between First and Second Avenues that the running joke is that they're all served by one huge underground kitchen. For a standout, head just around the corner to the gaudily bedecked Panna II at 93 First Ave. Just be sure to go up the stairs and to your right, as staff from the lesser joints downstairs and upstairs left will try very hard to convince you otherwise.

PRUNE Owned and run by top lesbian chef Gabrielle Hamilton, Prune is upscale East Village bohemia at its finest: fantastic new American food, understated art-hipster clientele, and enough Bloody Mary variations to turn the already magical weekend brunch into a serious party. 54 E. 1st St. (between First and Second Aves., map D1), 212-677-6221, PRUNERESTAURANT.COM **MODERATE**

LAVAGNA Despite being somewhat forgotten by critics (who lavished praise on it a few years back) as they move on to the next big thing, Lavagna is still going as strong and as excellent as ever, and its packed house proves it. Tucked away on an otherwise nondescript Alphabet City street, Lavagna's a diamond in the rough, offering amazing authentic-with-just-that-perfect-twist Italian that's unmatched for the price. Great warm ambience, too, making the close quarters hardly noticeable. 545 E. 5th St. (between Aves. A and B, map D2), 212-979-1005, LAVAGNA NYC.COM **MODERATE**

B & H DAIRY RESTAURANT Only in New York: Eastern European Jewish vegetarian, courtesy of B & H Dairy Restaurant. Local hipsters love the meat-freeness, neighborhood elders cherish the old world authenticity, and everyone loves the prices. 127 Second Ave. (between 7th St. and St. Marks Pl., map D3), 212-505-8065 **INEXPENSIVE**

MAMA'S FOOD SHOP Mother definitely stands for comfort at Mama's Food Shop, a no-frills neighborhood fave beloved as much for its ridiculously huge a la carte portions as its überartsy (but extremely friendly) East Village vibe. Choices run the gamut from healthy (grilled salmon, roasted Brussels sprouts) to not so much (meatloaf, mac and cheese). 200 E. 3rd St., (between Aves. A and B, map D4), 212-777-4425, MAMASFOODSHOP.COM/EAST **INEXPENSIVE**

SHOPPING

If you have time, it's well worth your shopping while to wander the streets on either side of St. Mark's Place for their bounty of great little boutiques. On 7th and 9th Streets they're especially good and plentiful.

KIEHL'S Visitors already giddy to have made it to the trendy Kiehl's brand's flagship store are always further wowed to learn that it's actually been in operation here for over 150 years, albeit originally as an apothecary. Check out the in-store Mudspot, serving excellent neighborhood-made brew Mud Coffee. 109 Third Ave. (at 13th St., map S1), 212-677-3171, KIEHLS.COM

ODIN Like the Norse god with which it shares a name, downtown clothier Odin is all about inspired wisdom, its deft assembly of

EAST VILLAGE GAY TIMELINE

1899 The Mazet Committee reports on "male degenerate" hangouts Columbia Hall (32 Cooper Square, between 5th and 6th Sts., map H1; also called Paresis Hall, a reference to syphilis) and Little Bucks across the street.

1916 Pressure from police raids on the gay-popular Lafayette Baths (403–405 Lafayette, between Astor Pl. and E. 4th St., map H2) leads to the suicide of the son of the owner, who sells the baths to George and Ira Gershwin's father; Ira later works here as a cashier, and it is also likely the setting for painter Charles Demuth's 1918 blatantly homoerotic self-portrait.

1920 Webster Hall (119 E. 11th St., between Third and Fourth Aves., map H3) hosts popular annual drag balls.

1953 Club 82 (82 E. 4th St., between Bowery and Second Ave., map H4) opens and reigns on the city's drag scene throughout the '50s and '60s, becoming a popular "wild side" spot with celebrities like Errol Flynn who reportedly enjoys playing the piano here without the use of his hands; in the early '70s the bar starts hosting rock shows by some of the most important pre-punk bands of the day, including The New York Dolls; in the '90s it will become a gay sex club.

EAST VILLAGE GAY TIMELINE

1978 Englishman in New York (the subject of Sting's song of the same name) and queer writer Quentin Crisp moves to 46 E. 3rd St. (at Second Ave., map H5) and lives here until his death in 1999.

1980 Male members-only megaclub The Saint (105 Second Ave., at 6th St., map H6) opens, and with its slate of wild and extravagant parties sets the stage for the country's gay circuit scene; in the former Fillmore East space, where countless top rock acts (including Janis Joplin, Jimi Hendrix, The Doors, and Led Zeppelin) played in the late '60s and early '70s.

1985 City officials shut down the New St. Marks Baths (6 St. Marks Pl., between Second and Third Aves., map H7) after inspectors witness what the *New York Times* reports were "50 acts of 'unsafe sex' involving more than 80 men."

1985 Lady Bunny launches the first Wigstock in Tompkins Square Park (map H8), where it draws a crowd of 1,000 in its first annual incarnation and 25,000 by 1993, its last year here before moving on to the Chelsea Piers, where it remained until 2001; in future years it would become part of the Howl! Festival, also held in Tompkins Square Park.

EAST VILLAGE GAY TIMELINE

1998   The original home of The Cock (188 Ave. A at 12th St., map H9) opens, bringing seven years of notorious rampant randiness to Alphabet City before its merge with The Hole and a move to Second Avenue in 2005.

2006   In an incident that sends shock waves through a gay New York that thought such horrors could no longer occur here, singer Kevin Aviance is attacked and brutally beaten (14th St., near First Ave.) by several youths after leaving The Phoenix. Four are arrested, and a valiant Aviance—jaw broken—insists on appearing in the year's Pride Parade just weeks later.

far-flung fashion-forward labels rendering it a one-stop stockist for the globe-trotting post-metrosexual. Brands include Comme des Garçons, Trovata, Y-3, Engineered Garments, and Rogues Gallery, but the stock (also featuring scents, sunglasses, and shoes) rotates regularly. Check out next-door Den too, where the same owners highlight one designer every six weeks or so. 328 E. 11th St. (between First and Second Aves., map S2), 212-475-0666, ODINNEWYORK.COM

OTHER MUSIC Across the street from the infamous but now defunct Tower Records's flagship, this indie-lover's utopia is the downtown arbiter of what's worth listening to right now, with a tapped-in staff that's eager to help. 15 E. 4th St. (between Broadway and Lafayette St., map S3), 212-477-8150, OTHERMUSIC.COM

ST. MARK'S BOOKSHOP The last great holdout among a dying breed in the neighborhood, St. Mark's Bookshop is a thinking man's paradise, offering up the highest brow in history, fiction, philosophy, and culture for 30 years and counting. 31 Third Ave. (at 9th St., map S4), 212-260-7853, STMARKSBOOKSHOP.COM

ST. MARK'S PLACE Locals avoid it like the plague for its tourist and NYU-er overrun, but this crowded gateway to the East Village, especially between Second and Third Avenues (map S5), is lined with fairly decent bargain shops catering mostly to, well, tourists and NYU-ers.

NIGHTLIFE

A good number of the city's more happening alterna-gays may now call places like Williamsburg home, but the East Village is still New York's go-to gay hipster party enclave.

BEIGE (TUESDAYS ONLY) The long-running and always packed Beige is a Tuesday night must for the city's upmarket homo hipster set. B Bar, 40 E. 4th St. (at Bowery, map N1), 212-475-2222, BBARANDGRILL.COM

THE BOILER ROOM Having once reigned supreme on the East Village scene, the Boiler Room has taken (and become) a dive, but it's still good for no-frills fun. 86 E. 4th St. (between First and Second Aves., map N2), 212-254-7536

BOYSROOM (MONDAYS ONLY) The naughty BoysRoom has left its former space down the street to take up Monday night residence at Rapture Café. 200 Ave. A (between 12th and 13th Sts., map N3), 212-228-1177, MYSPACE.COM/BOYSROOM

IN THE STEPS OF ALLEN GINSBERG

Poet, radical, Beat generation godfather, and gay icon, Allen Ginsberg was also a lover of the East Village, living in the area for the better part of 40 years, when he wasn't off busy being deported from Cuba or earning the tag of "immoral menace" from the Czechoslovakian government.

Born in New Jersey in 1926, Ginsberg attended Columbia University before moving to the East Village in 1952, living until the following year at **206 EAST 7TH STREET** (between Aves. B and C, map P1) with roommates Gregory Corso and William Burroughs (who reportedly began writing *Naked Lunch* here). This was where Ginsberg shot many photographs of Burroughs and Jack Kerouac, including a classic fire escape shot of the latter. After a few important years in San Francisco, Ginsberg returned to the East Village, setting up camp with lover Peter Orlovsky at **170 EAST 2ND STREET** (between Aves. A and B, map P2) from 1958 to '61. Here he wrote *Kaddish* (considered one of his best works) and hosted at least

THE COCK Having long raised high hell on Avenue A, The Cock is now up to its same nefarious hijinx over on Second Avenue. 29 Second Ave. (between 1st and 2nd Sts., map N4), 212-777-6254

EASTERN BLOC Manhattan's most modish 'mos flock to small coolspot Eastern Bloc (formerly Wonder Bar), always lively and crammed to capacity on weekends. 505 E. 6th St. (between Aves. A and B, map N5), 212-777-2555, EASTERNBLOCNYC.COM

IN THE STEPS OF ALLEN GINSBERG

one early and seminal psychedelic party when Timothy Leary paid a visit. In the late '60s/early '70s Ginsberg lived at **408 EAST 10TH STREET** (between Aves. C and D, map P3), then in 1975, moved to **437 EAST 12TH STREET** (between First Ave. and Ave. A, map P4), where he lived most of the rest of his life. A few blocks away, Ginsberg was a witness to the 1988 police riot in Tompkins Square Park, which fittingly two decades later is now the site of the Howl! Festival, named for Ginsberg's most famous work.

Having early on been filled with "whole mountains of homosexuality" (as he put it in *Kaddish*), Ginsberg lived his life openly and freely in a pre-Stonewall era when few dared to do so, and was among other things the first Who's Who entrant to list a same-sex partner. He died in his beloved East Village in 1997. "The young people who moved to this neighborhood two years ago don't know what Ginsberg has done for it," Orlovsky told the *New York Times.*

NOWHERE Nowhere is so named so you won't find it, lest you disturb the nice hipsters as they mingle in this friendly and very cozy drink den. 212-477-4744, GAYBARSNYC.COM

THE PHOENIX Nabe mainstay The Phoenix is always occupied by a friendly and low maintenance crowd, plus it's got the city's best jukebox. 447 E. 13th St. (between 1st Ave. and Ave. A, map N7), 212-477-9979, GAYBARSNYC.COM

URGE Whether owing to its former existence as a funeral parlor or to its sex clubby aroma, Urge has a darkish feel, but it boasts a bevy of pumped up bar-top strippers and is always cruisey and crowded. 33 Second Ave. (between 1st and 2nd Sts., map N8), 212-533-5757, THEURGENYC.COM

LOWER EAST SIDE

For most of its life playing home to successive waves of the city's most poor and marginalized, the Lower East Side was the home turf of freed blacks in the 1820s, Irish famine fleers in the 1840s, Germans in the 1850s, and Italians in the 1870s before a massive influx of Eastern European Jews arrived between the 1880s and 1920s. After World War II came Puerto Ricans in large numbers, providing a key element of the modern Lower East Side character.

In the early 1990s, gentrification began pushing both south from the East Village and east from SoHo, culminating in a neighborhood that is today if not Manhattan's hippest, certainly the one with the most hipster street cred. Downtown trendy shops and restaurants share blocks with old school businesses and bodegas, giving the area a decidedly vibrant flair. On weekend nights, the Lower East Side's streets (especially around Rivington and Stanton) are now literally awash with sauced-up (mostly straight and white) youngfolk.

ACTIVITIES

LOWER EAST SIDE TENEMENT MUSEUM America's first preserved homestead of the urban working class, the amazing Lower East Side Tenement Museum is visited by more than 100,000 people a year. The building itself is estimated to have housed a staggering 7,000 tenants between 1863 and 1935. Guided tours only, book ahead. $17, open Tu–F 1–5, Sa–Su 11–4:45. 108 Orchard St. (between Delancey and Broome Sts., map A6), 212-431-0233, TENEMENT.ORG

NEW MUSEUM This stunningly original new home to the 30-year-old New Museum opened in late 2007, heralding what many believe is the shift in focus for the city's contemporary art scene from Chelsea to the Lower East Side. $12, open W, Sa, and Su 12–6, Th–F 12–10. 235 Bowery (between Stanton and Rivington Sts., map A7), 212-219-1222, NEWMUSEUM.ORG

SEE ALSO IN FILM: Landmark Sunshine Cinema
SEE ALSO IN MUSIC: Bowery Ballroom

LODGING

BLUE MOON A former tenement building painstakingly converted into a 1930s/'40s-themed luxury hotel, Blue Moon boasts (relative to the city average) large rooms (starting at 320 square feet), each named for a celeb from the era (e.g., James Cagney, Fanny Brice, and Milton Berle). It's on the steep end of the price scale, but it's uniquely fancy and fanciful, and it's a terrific luxe launching point for exploring the increasingly trendy Lower East Side (the Tenement Museum is right next door), as well as the nearby East

LOWER EAST SIDE GAY TIMELINE

1899 The Mazet Committee reports on "male degenerate" hangout the Palm Club (Chrystie Street).

Village, Nolita, and Chinatown environs. 100 Orchard St. (between Delancey and Broome Sts., map L5), 212-533-9080, BLUEMOON-NYC.COM **EXPENSIVE**

DINING

SCHILLER'S LIQUOR BAR Don't let the name fool you: Schiller's caters to more than merely those seeking pickling. Another Keith McNally brainchild, Schiller's offers high-end eclectic wee-hour comfort to hungry Lower East Side hipsters. Open till 3 A M on weekends. 131 Rivington St. (at Norfolk St., map D5), 212-260-4555, SCHILLERSNY.COM **MODERATE**

CLINTON STREET BAKING COMPANY Lower East Side hipsters may form its base crowd, but Clinton Street Baking Company was recently voted by all *Time Out New York* readers as the city's best brunch spot. Basically a glorified diner, the vibe is very friendly, and the food is scrumptious comfort incarnate. It's just the wait that could suck. 4 Clinton St. (at Houston St., map D6), 646-602-6263, GREATBISCUITS.COM **MODERATE**

SHOPPING

BBLESSING While ostensibly the coolest men's clothing shop on the Lower East Side (carrying such "bleeding edge" lines as Raf Simons, Rag & Bone, Preen, and Giacometti), BBlessing is also a purveyor of such other modern day dandy lifestyle staples as übereclectic books and DVDs. The ever-evolving refined-cum-artfully-skewed interior includes such unique appointments as a dazzling crack pipe chandelier. 181 Orchard St. (at Stanton St., map S6), 212-378-8005, BBLESSING.COM

BLUESTOCKINGS Its name culled from a 19th-century term for women with strong literary interests, radical bookstore/fair trade café/activist center Bluestockings carries over 4,500 titles, with special concentration on feminist and queer studies. 172 Allen St. (between Stanton and Rivington Sts., map S7), 212-777-6028, BLUESTOCKINGS.COM

CHELSEA, UNION SQUARE, AND GRAMERCY

CHELSEA

Taking its name from the family estate of Clement Moore (he of *'Twas the Night Before Christmas* fame) that once stood at the heart of the modern day hood, Chelsea has, like much of New York City, known several very different incarnations. Pastoral early on in a couple of senses—Moore gave farmland to help establish the General Theological Seminary, which in 1827 began building the complex which still occupies the block between 20th and 21st Streets and Ninth and Tenth Avenues—Chelsea's rural charm was forever disrupted by the Hudson River Railroad tracks that were laid in the late 1840s along what is today Tenth and Eleventh Avenues, slicing off access to the waterfront. The rail lines and adjoining dock yards brought a flood of Irish immigrants to the area, the majority of whom lived in the many tenements thrown up to meet the wave.

Though it was home for a century to the Everard Baths (known to many as the Ever-Hard Baths, one of the city's more notorious gay-popular bathhouses) and starting in the 1970s to manly men bars The Spike, The Eagle, and The Glory Hole, Chelsea didn't morph into a true gay mecca until the late '80s and early '90s, when those fleeing rising West Village rents looked northward and found a neighborhood ready for dramatic transformation. So complete now is the shift that New York PrideFest organizers have petitioned the city (so far unsuccessfully) to move the annual post-Gay Pride festival from the West Village to Chelsea. The nabe's gay fame has even brought it (if not entirely fairly) into the queer lexicon in the guise of the Chelsea Queen, a stereotypical (if not steroidical) pumped-up gym and partygoer.

In the 1990s, Chelsea became an upstart art center and rapidly replaced SoHo as the gallery capital of Manhattan, eventually boasting more than 200 of them. Lately far west Chelsea has become an especially hot gallery zone, despite recent rumblings of a possible further mass shift to the Lower East Side. The gays, meanwhile, have already begun meandering further northward to Hell's Kitchen (which many call Hellsea), though no one believes that'll un-gay Chelsea anytime soon. For now, it remains the artiest and faggiest (but not the art-faggiest) few-block radius in New York, if not the world.

ACTIVITIES

Along the same rail stretch that once cut Chelsea off from the waterfront, the much ballyhooed High Line (THEHIGHLINE.ORG) will open its first phase of inner-city green space in Summer 2008, and is destined to become one of the neighborhood's most popular attractions. Meanwhile there's plenty to keep one busy beyond the obligatory boywatching.

CHELSEA ART MUSEUM Once you grow weary from looking at art you can't afford at the slew of nearby galleries, take a breather at the Chelsea Art Museum, where you can rest assured that nothing's for sale. A 30,000 square foot space devoted to showcasing important international artists who've previously received little exposure stateside, the museum is also home to the Miotte Foundation, which conserves the work of the French Informel movement proponent Jean Miotte. $6, open Tu–Sa noon–6 (Th till 8). 556 West 22nd St. (between Tenth and Eleventh Aves., map A1), 212-255-0719, CHELSEARTMUSEUM.ORG

CHELSEA PIERS A fairly astounding 28-acre sports encampment jutting into the Hudson River between 17th and 23rd Streets, Chelsea Piers offers a massive golf club, ice rinks, a bowling center, a health club, a full-service spa, and a field house with baseball, basketball, soccer, and gymnastics facilities. Piers 59 to 62 (map A2), 212-336-6666, CHELSEAPIERS.COM

THE MUSEUM AT FIT Founded 40 years ago as a learning resource for Fashion Institute of Technology students, the Museum at FIT is one of the world's few fashion-only museums, housing one of the most important fashion and textile collections anywhere. Watch for a devoted Accessories Collection, in the works via a $1 million donation in 2005 from the estate of a high fashion hat distributor. Free, open Tu–F noon–8, Sa 10–5. Seventh Ave. at 27th St. (map A3), 212-217-4558, FITNYC.EDU/MUSEUM

RUBIN MUSEUM As the Western World's first museum dedicated to Himalayan and adjacent art, the Rubin boasts a gorgeous collection of Tibetan, Indian, Chinese, Bhutanese, Mongolian, and Nepalese works, lovingly presented throughout six floors of a section of the former Barneys flagship store. $10, open M and Th 11–5, W 11–7, F 11–10, Sa–Su 11–6). 150 W. 17th St. (between Sixth and Seventh Aves., map A4), 212-620-5000, RMANYC.ORG

CHELSEA GAY TIMELINE

1969 Energized by Stonewall and inspired by other counterculture movements, radical gays break away from the homophile movement to form the Gay Liberation Front, holding its first meeting at Alternate U (69 W. 14th St., at Sixth Ave., map H1)

1975 Gay bar Mother's (267 W. 23rd St., between Seventh and Eighth Aves., map H2) becomes a powerhouse on the early American punk music scene with performers including The Ramones, Blondie, and Talking Heads.

1977 A fire at the Everard Baths (28 W. 28th St. at Broadway, map H3) kills nine people; the blaze is later called "inevitable" because of the "disgusting" conditions inside the macho men's bathhouse.

1978 Inspired by the gay fun long known to be available at the McBurney Y (215 W. 23rd St., between Seventh and Eighth Aves., map H4; since moved to 14th St.), the Village People come out with "YMCA."

1979 Part of William Friedkin's *Cruising* is shot at notorious gay haunt the Eagle's Nest (142 Eleventh Ave. at 21st St., map H5) before protests cause the bar to ban Friedkin from the premises.

CHELSEA GAY TIMELINE

1989 The Sound Factory (12 W. 21st St., between Fifth and Sixth Aves., map H6) opens, and will become a critical player in the development of garage and house music, vaulting Junior Vasquez and Little Louie Vega into dance music stardom; it had been gay video bar Private Eyes, where Madonna and Sean Penn went on their first date; later it became Cheetah.

1989 Gay Saturdays at The Roxy (515 W. 18th St. at Tenth Ave., map H7) begin, and will dominate the gay dance scene throughout the '90s and into the '00s before ceasing in 2007.

SEE ALSO IN ART: Andrea Rosen Gallery, Daniel Reich Gallery, Matthew Marks Gallery

SEE ALSO IN DANCE: Dance Theater Workshop, Joyce Theater, The Kitchen

SEE ALSO IN MUSIC: Highline Ballroom

LODGING

Not traditionally abundant with temporary accommodations, Chelsea, like many parts of the city, is experiencing something of a hotel boom. Several interesting new properties are slated to open soon, including New York City's first Hotel Indigo at 127 W. 28th St. (between Sixth and Seventh Aves.) in late 2008.

THE MARITIME Though its unchallenged "it" status of the mid-naughts has passed to newer comers like the Gramercy Park and The Bowery, The Maritime is still a great choice and for now still the chicest in Chelsea. Sean MacPherson and Eric Goode turned this striking building, once the National Maritime Union headquarters, into the present nautically themed hotel, which opened in 2003. Great views of the Hudson River, and downstairs club Hiro hosts the trendy gay Cuckoo Club on Sunday nights. 363 W. 16th St. (at Ninth Ave., map L1), 212-242-4300, THEMARITIMEHOTEL.COM **EXPENSIVE**

HOTEL CHELSEA A city landmark for 125 years, the Chelsea has served as permanent or temporary home to a steady stream of famous and infamous creative types, from Mark Twain to Dylan Thomas to Edie Sedgwick to Sid Vicious and girlfriend Nancy Spungen, who in 1978 lost her life in Room 100. Long revered by bohemian travelers for its extant spirits of artists past and present, the Chelsea is currently undergoing an uncertain shift, having in mid-'07, to the dismay of nearly everyone, booted longtime managers the Bard family, and called in the same team that manages hipster-chic properties like The Mercer in SoHo. Promises have been made that charm will be respected and preserved, but no one's holding their breath. Our advice: Stay here now while there's still ambience for the soaking. 222 W. 23rd St. (between Seventh and Eighth Aves., map L2), 212-243-3700, HOTELCHELSEA.COM **MODERATE**

CHELSEA PINES INN For economy of both pocketbook and locale, gay-owned 26-room guesthouse Chelsea Pines Inn is a wise choice, with very affordable rates and a setting smack at the juncture of Chelsea, the West Village, and the Meatpacking District. The cheapest rooms share a toilet, but all have their own sink and shower, and the still reasonably priced deluxe model now comes with flat-screen TV, iPod dock, and the like following a major property-wide revamp in 2007. 317 W. 14th St. (between Eighth and Ninth Aves., map L3), 212-929-1023 or 888-546-2700, CHELSEAPINESINN.COM **MODERATE**

CHELSEA LODGE Don't be daunted by the rusty Web site: Chelsea Lodge consistently receives high praise from former guests for its dirt-cheap rates, its clean and comfortable (if small) rooms, and its endearingly quirky staff. For some reason, it's especially popular with budget-minded Eurogays. For a bit more space for just a few more bucks, check out the neighboring Chelsea Lodge Suites (CHELSEALODGESUITES.COM). 318 W. 20th St. (between Eighth and Ninth Aves., map L4), 212-243-4499 or 800-373-1116, CHELSEALODGE.COM **INEXPENSIVE**

DINING

The dual influx of gays and arties to Chelsea in recent years has naturally brought along the requisite plethora of fabulous dining options, one of Manhattan's two Olive Garden outlets notwithstanding.

COOKSHOP A blithe blend of *depeche mode* refined and down home relaxed, Cookshop is the sort of place you know you'll come back to, both for the invigorating ambience and the impeccable American food. Owner/chef Marc Meyers, also proprietor of NoHo's Five Points, favors locally grown and humanely raised ingredients like Montauk squid and Catskill duck. The menu changes often, but a constant (and constant surprise favorite) is the fried spiced hominy. 156 Tenth Ave. (at 20th St., map D1), 212-944-4440, COOK SHOPNY.COM **EXPENSIVE**

IN THE STEPS OF MEL CHEREN

When the newly formed Gay Men's Health Crisis went looking for its first home in 1982, no one would rent to the AIDS-fighting organization. No one, that is, except Mel Cheren, who not only provided the space in his brownstone at **318 WEST 22ND STREET** (between Eighth and Ninth Aves., map P1), but also refused to accept rent for the first year. After the group moved on to bigger quarters in 1984, Cheren turned the building into the Colonial House Inn (colonialhouseinn.com), a gay-popular B&B still satisfying budget-conscious travelers to New York City, and where he himself lived the rest of his life.

Massachusetts-born Cheren was often called "The Godfather of Disco," having founded West End Records and produced such '70s dance megahits as Karen Young's "Hot Shot" and Taana Gardner's "Heartbeat." Active on the New York/Fire Island club circuit of the day, Cheren had his finger on the dance pulse, and was the idea man behind

BUDDAKAN Pegged by *New York* magazine as one of the 10 best new restaurants for 2007, Buddakan is a Philadelphia transplant, blending old school Asian with incredible innovation (e.g., the taro puff lollipops) served amidst a gorgeously trendy (and fairly massive) venue at one end of Chelsea Market. 75 Ninth Ave. (between 15th and 16th Sts., map D2), 212-989-6699, BUDDAKANNYC.COM **EXPENSIVE**

IN THE STEPS OF MEL CHEREN

no less than the 12-inch disco single, the instrumental B-side, and the scratching sound that eventually became a hip-hop DJ mainstay. In 1977 he put up the cash to launch the fabled Paradise Garage on King Street in SoHo, which reigned supreme on the black/Latin/gay club scene for the next decade.

In 2000, Cheren's cowrote *My Life and the Paradise Garage: Keep On Dancin'*, chronicling his experiences as a gay man in New York City from the late 1950s on through to Stonewall-era liberation, disco debauchery, and the ensuing AIDS nightmare, during which he lost countless friends and associates. Profits from the book went to his charity 24 Hours for Life, dedicated to raising money from the music industry for AIDS relief. Cheren remained active on the music scene until his final days, when in December 2007 at the age of 74 he lost his final battle with HIV.

EAST OF EIGHTH A neighborhood gay favorite, East of Eighth serves an eclectic American cuisine with hints of Asian, Indian, and Italian. For those bound for the Theater District or a Madison Square Garden event (or for just anyone who has early evening hunger pangs), the three course Dinner at Dusk is a popular option. 254 W. 23rd St. (between Seventh and Eighth Aves., map D3), 212-352-0075, EASTOFEIGHTH.COM **MODERATE**

CAFETERIA If it's consistently great food or always friendly service you seek, go elsewhere. But for a fun and scene-y mixed/gay vibe, usually tasty comfort fare, and the occasional model/celeb sighting, all available 24 hours a day, look no further than Cafeteria. 119 Seventh Ave. (at 17th St., map D4), 212-414-1717 **MODERATE**

SHOPPING

BARNEYS CO-OP It may not be nearly as big as the original Barneys flagship store that once stood around the corner, but this was the brand's first ever Co-op outlet, and it still offers the very hippest in young menswear around. 236 West 18th St. (between Seventh and Eighth Aves., map S1), 212-593-7800, BARNEYS.COM

CHELSEA MARKET A foodie's paradise, Chelsea Market is an upscale indoor bazaar selling fine edibles, drinkables, cookware, flowers, and gifts; it's also a hyper-hip food court with several excellent dining options; it's also great for boywatching, especially on weekends when groovy locals stock up here. Upstairs in the vast complex (part of Nabisco's old headquarters and where the Oreo was actually born) are the Food Network's offices and studios. 75 Ninth Ave. (between 15th and 16th Sts., map S2), CHELSEAMARKET.COM

COMME DES GARÇONS It's fitting that Comme des Garçons is set smack among Chelsea's galleries, since Japanese fashion-forward torchbearing designer Rei Kawakubo's clothes are perennially art in and of themselves. Her signature unisex scents are divine too. 520 W. 22nd St. (between Tenth and Eleventh Aves., map S3), 212-604-9200

NASTY PIG Release your inner dirty leather daddy at this respected and recently renovated haberdashery for the macho man. 265A W.

19th St. (between Seventh and Eighth Aves., map S4), 212-691-6067, NASTYPIG.COM

NIGHTLIFE

Chelsea's nightlife options run the gay gamut from the rugged (the ever-raunchy Rawhide and Eagle) to the athletic (GYM Sportsbar) to the polished on up to the downright fabulous (Cuckoo Club).

BARRACUDA Voted by *HX* magazine as 2007's Best Bar in New York, Barracuda is arguably the least Chelsea-ish of Chelsea's bars, with a cool and fun anything-can-happen sort of vibe not usually found outside the East Village (or maybe more recently Hell's Kitchen). 275 W. 22nd St. (at Eighth Ave., map N1), 212-645-8613

CUCKOO CLUB (SUNDAYS ONLY) Huge and wildly popular Sundays club scene spectacular. Hiro Ballroom, Maritime Hotel, 371 W. 16th St. (between Eighth and Ninth Aves., map N2), 212-727-0212, MYSPACE.COM/CUCKOOCLUBNYC

THE EAGLE Leather and Levis rule the roost at this cruisey and friendly man-haunt. 554 W. 28th St. (between Tenth and Eleventh Aves., map N3), 646-473-1866, EAGLENYC.COM

G LOUNGE The preferred lounge of upscale Chelseadom. 225 W. 19th St. (between Seventh and Eighth Aves., map N4), 212-929-1085, GLOUNGE.COM

GYM SPORTSBAR The city's first and only gay sports bar. 167 Eighth Ave. (between 18th and 19th Sts., map N5), 212-337-2439, GYMSPORTSBAR.COM

RAWHIDE Mature leathermen and bears roam at this Chelsea institution. 212 Eighth Ave. (at 21st St., map N6), 212-242-9332

SPLASH Chelsea's legendary big naughty dance bar. 50 W. 17th St. (between Fifth and Sixth Aves., map N7), 212-691-0073, SPLASHBAR.COM

XES LOUNGE A popular and attitude-free happy hour hangout with a smoking patio. 157 W. 24th St (between Sixth and Seventh Aves., map N8), 212-604-0212, XESLOUNGE.COM

UNION SQUARE

Once a burial ground for the city's poor, Union Square (so named for being the place where Broadway met Bowery, now Fourth Ave.) was opened as a public park in 1839, and would become an important center for public meetings and rallies throughout the nineteenth century. In 1882 it played a key role in the first Labor Day celebration, and nearly a century later, in 1970, it did the same during the first Earth Day festivities. Following the terrorist attacks of September 11, 2001, it also served as a main public gathering area for mourners. Since the mid '70s the square has probably been most famous for its Greenmarket (see below), but with its pleasant open spaces and union of many subway lines below, it's also a very popular downtown meeting spot for locals. In the month leading up to Christmas, the Union Square Holiday Market annually fills the park with seasonal cheer as more than a hundred booths (open daily) sell unique gifts and decorations.

ACTIVITY

UNION SQUARE GREENMARKET Serving upwards of a quarter million customers a week at peak times, this three-decades-old open-air city institution lets upstate and New England area farmers hawk their produce to a hungry and very appreciative big city. Open M, W, F, and Sa 8am–6pm. Map A5.

LODGING

HOTEL 17 Budget-minded hipsters love Hotel 17, where a tradeoff in creature comforts (the mostly shared-bath accommodations are a tad weathered, albeit passably well kept) is amply compensated for via price, locale (a mere stone's throw from the East Village),

MADISON SQUARE PARK, EARLY EVENING

UNION SQUARE GAY TIMELINE

1901 The Committee of Fifteen, an antigambling and prostitution watchdog group, reports finding 75 "fairies" in the back room of Billy's Hotel (Third Ave. near 20th St., map H8) one spring evening, "dressed as women" with low necklines, short skirts, and blond wigs. In a police raid the same year at the nearby Sharon Hotel (136 Third Ave., between 14th and 15th Sts., map H9), which is known in the neighborhood as "Cock Suckers Hall," the *New York Times* reports that 52 people are taken into custody, and three men are eventually "sent to the island for six months" after being charged with "extraordinary depravity."

1968 In one of the most notorious recorded cases of dyke-on-fag aggression, Valerie Solanas shoots Andy Warhol three times at The Factory (33 Union Square West, Sixth Floor, map H10).

and downtown-cool bragging rights (Madonna once dwelled here, and club scene queen Amanda LePore still does). 225 E. 17th St. (between Second and Third Aves., map L5), 212-475-2845, HOTEL17NY.COM **INEXPENSIVE**

DINING

UNION SQUARE CAFÉ Though it's often noted for its gorgeous staff who, though friendly, would pretty clearly rather be modeling and/or acting, the real star at this very popular gem is the food, flawless American fare with an Italian flair. While properly pricey, this is the epitome of urbane urban casual. 21 E. 16th St. (between Union Square West and Fifth Ave., map D5), 212-243-4020, UNIONSQUARECAFE.COM **EXPENSIVE**

BITE Serving superb sandwiches, salads, and soups at serious savings (whole meals under $10), Bite's a fave among local penny-pinching gastronomes. The Middle Eastern turkey sandwich gets especially high praise. 211 E. 14th St. (between Second and Third Aves., map D6), 212-677-3123 **INEXPENSIVE**

SHOPPING

Literally surrounded by power chains including Virgin Megastore, Circuit City, Sephora, TJ Maxx, Filene's Basement, Whole Foods, and Trader Joe's, Union Square is also at the base of a home décor shopping alley lining Broadway up to 23rd Street.

ABC CARPET & HOME Despite its quirky (and fairly misleading) name, ABC Carpet is actually a sprawling six floor paradise of high-end furnishings for the entire home. Hip locals appoint their pads here with the best in everything big to small, floor to ceiling, bed to bath, and antique to modern. 888 Broadway (at 19th St., map S5), 212-473-3000, ABCHOME.COM

GRAMERCY

Garnering its name (via corrupted Dutch) from a crooked brook that used to flow along modern day 21st Street, Gramercy is a quiet and largely upscale residential neighborhood with boundaries that are hard to define. To some Gramercy occupies the entire region from 14th Street to 30th Street and from Fifth Avenue to the East River, but many, especially area residents themselves, would argue that vehemently. What is certain is that at Gramercy's historic and physical heart lies the park of the same name, which is so tied to the area's identity that the neighborhood itself is often mistakenly called Gramercy Park. Built in 1831, the park has been private ever since, making it the only remaining one of its kind in Manhattan and the oldest in the country. Only residents of surrounding buildings have keys, making there three ways to get in: befriend one of said residents, stay at the Gramercy Park Hotel, or go on the one day a year the park is opened to common riffraff like you.

ACTIVITY

MUSEUM OF SEX Playfully stretching the boundaries of both Gramercy and modesty, the Museum of Sex (MoSex) uses a variety of media to explore the history and cultural magnitude of human sexuality. $14.50+tax, open Su–F 11–6:30, Sa 11–8. 233 Fifth Ave. (at 27th St., map A6), 212-689-6337, MUSEUMOFSEX.COM

LODGING

GRAMERCY PARK Opened to much fanfare in 2006, the Ian Schrager-renovated Gramercy Park is one of the reigning lords of New York hotel überhipdom. Though *laissez-faire* locals (loyal fans of its former rundown charm) still bemoan the loss of the old property, there's little denying that the new Gramercy Park is tremendously fabulous in a very late-naughts kind of way. Gone is the hallmark Philippe Starck minimalism of previous Schrager efforts; in its place, Julian Schnabel's wacky but somehow supremely elegant mashing of far-flung design elements. The city's top scenesters imbibe at the Rose Bar downstairs. Oh, and Jude Law has been known to bunk here. 2 Lexington Ave. (between 21st and 22nd Sts., map L), 212-920-3300 or 866-784-1300, GRAMERCYPARKHOTEL.COM
EXPENSIVE

DINING

GRAMERCY TAVERN Though it stumbled a bit when souper-star Tom Colicchio left in late 2006, Gramercy Tavern is back in perfect form under the helm of new chef Michael Anthony, whose fare is noticeably lighter and higher concept than Colicchio's famed haute hearty grub. The atmosphere is sophisticated but relaxed, and the superb *prix fixe* dinners are relative culinary bargains. 42 E. 20th St. (between Broadway and Park Ave. South, map D7), 212-477-0777, GRAMERCYTAVERN.COM **EXPENSIVE**

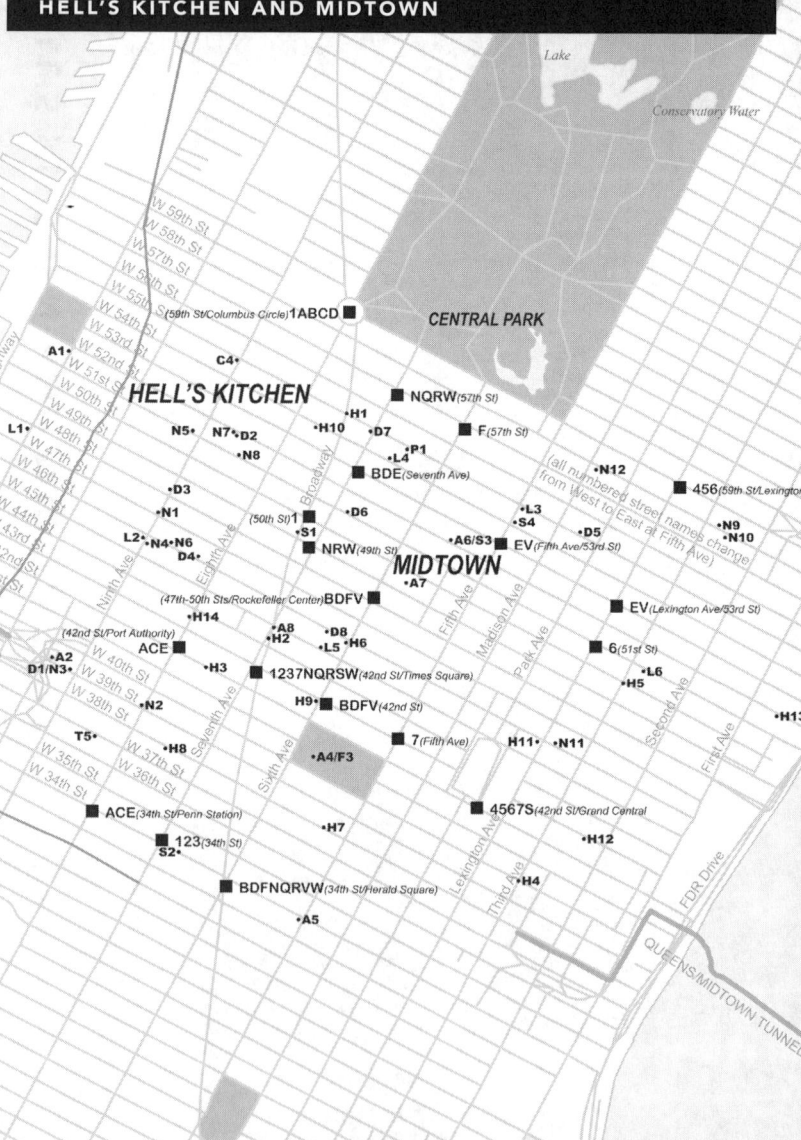

Lake

Conservatory Water

CENTRAL PARK

1ABCD (59th St/Columbus Circle)

A1•

C4•

HELL'S KITCHEN

NQRW (57th St)

N5• N7•D2 •H10 •D7 •H1 F (57th St)

L1• L4• P1

•N8 BDE (Seventh Ave)

•D3

•N1 (50th St) 1 •D6 •N12 456 (59th St/Lexington A

L2• N4•N6 •S1 •L3 •N9

D4• NRW (49th St) •S4 •N10

•A6/S3 •D5

MIDTOWN EV (Fifth Ave/53rd St)

(47th-50th Sts/Rockefeller Center) BDFV •A7

•H14 EV (Lexington Ave/53rd St)

(42nd St/Port Authority) •A8 •D8

ACE •H2 •L5 •H6 6 (51st St)

•A2 •H3 1237NQRSW (42nd St/Times Square) •L6

D1/N3• •H5

•N2 H9• BDFV (42nd St) •H13

T5• 7 (Fifth Ave) H11• •N11

•H8 •A4/F3

ACE (34th St/Penn Station) 4567S (42nd St/Grand Central

123 (34th St) •H12

S2• •H7

BDFNQRVW (34th St/Herald Square) •H4

•A5

QUEENS/MIDTOWN TUNNEL

(all numbered street names change from West to East at Fifth Ave)

FDR Drive

HELL'S KITCHEN

Also known (but less so these days) as Clinton, Hell's Kitchen is the most recently settled of the city's gay enclaves, earning it the new monikers of Hellsea and NoChe, both nods to southern neighbor Chelsea ("Hell's Kitchenette" and "Hell's Pantry" are other favorites). Running roughly from 34th to 57th Streets and from Eighth Avenue west to the Hudson River, Hell's Kitchen's proximity to Broadway and the Theater District has meant stray gays have long lived here, attracted by the formerly cheap rents of its tenement-style housing. It's only in the past few years though that gay people (mostly men) have settled here *en bloc,* bringing with them the requisite bars and restaurants that now make Hellsea arguably the city's hottest homo haunt.

Hell's Kitchen got its inauspicious start as a Hudson River-adjacent shantytown in the mid-1800s, serving as home to the countless Potato Famine-fleeing Irish immigrants who found work along the area's docks and rail lines. When the local population ballooned after the Civil War, tenements shot up and gang-style crime skyrocketed. It's during this period that a cop called Dutch Fred reportedly uttered the phrase that's most commonly credited with giving the area its name, in response to his partner who'd commented on the nabe's similarity to Satan's underworld kingdom. "Hell's a mild climate," allegedly said Fred. "This is Hell's Kitchen."

In the early 20th century, Prohibition only fueled the violence and racketeering in the neighborhood. The booming post–World War II economy brought relative calm and prosperity as a new wave of immigrants from Puerto Rico came to live and work alongside the Irish—if not always entirely peacefully, as famously depicted on stage and screen in *West Side Story*.

Today's Hell's Kitchen is one of the most nationalistically diverse neighborhoods in the city, with Peruvians, Ecuadorians, Germans, and Eastern Europeans among those who are represented strongly. The recent gay influx looks set not to replace this mix whole hog as happened in Chelsea, but to coexist peacefully as just the latest element in a rich, feisty, and sometimes downright devilish stew.

ACTIVITIES

While it's just a stone's throw from such major Manhattan attractions as Times Square and the Theater District, Hell's Kitchen proper doesn't exactly overflow with its own must-see tourist sites, but it does harbor a few gems.

THE DAILY SHOW WITH JON STEWART STUDIO ABANDON NEWS, ALL YE WHO ENTER HERE warns a sign above the door to this home of the Comedy Central smash. When it's in production, *The Daily* tapes Mondays to Thursdays at 6:30 PM; book tickets well in advance, as studio space is limited. 733 Eleventh Ave. (between 51st and 52nd Sts., map A1), tickets 212-586-2477, THEDAILYSHOW.COM/TICKETS.JHTML

HELL'S KITCHEN FLEA MARKET Open every Saturday and Sunday year round, this quirky hodgepodge of antiques, vintage clothing, and other collectibles has been going strong for over 30 years, and brings in locals, tourists, artists, and celebrities alike. 39th St. (between Ninth and Tenth Aves., map A2), HELLSKITCHENFLEAMARKET.COM

INTREPID SEA-AIR-SPACE MUSEUM Unquestionably one of Hell's Kitchen's most enduring sightseeing attractions, the mighty Intrepid is set to reopen in Fall 2008 after two years of extensive renovations. Annually in late May the former U.S. Navy aircraft carrier hosts a roster of events related to Fleet Week, seven days that always make the local boys especially glad they live in Hellsea. Pier 86, Twelfth Ave. and 46th St. (map A3), 212-245-0072, INTREPIDMUSEUM.ORG

SEE ALSO IN DANCE: Joan Weill Center for Dance
SEE ALSO IN THEATER: Zipper Factory Theatre

LODGING

VU HOTEL Debuting mid-2008 to much area excitement, the Kimpton Group's $125 million 16-story Vu Hotel offers incredible views of the Hudson River and Times Square from its 222 rooms, and is expected to be just the first in a parade of high-end Hellsea inns. To boot, like all Kimptons it's pet friendly, so Mr. Barky von Schnauzer needn't stay behind. 653 Eleventh Ave. (at 48th St.), 212-757-0088 or 877-843-8869, VUHOTEL.COM **EXPENSIVE**

HOTEL 414 For a bit of style and an address at the heart of the 'hood, the cozy Hotel 414 has the further plus (or minus, depending on how much you want to mingle with fellow tourists) of being right along Restaurant Row. Book far ahead, as the 22 rooms fill quickly. 414 W. 46th St. (at Ninth Ave.), 212-399-0006 or 866-414-HOTEL, HOTEL414.COM **MODERATE**

DINING

The pink incursion into the neighborhood has naturally brought shamelessly gay dining to the table, among the more popular (and fortunately better) of this ilk being the French-Asian HK and the Asian-Asian Bamboo 52. Thanks to its mix of mingling nationalities, Hell's Kitchen also offers a vast bounty of small under-the-radar dining options, many of which take part in the wonderful International Food Festival that commandeers Ninth Avenue between 37th and 57th Streets the weekend after Mother's Day every year.

BAMBOO 52 Sleekly serving up sushi, sashimi, soups, salads, and saketinis, Bamboo 52 is a Hell's Kitchen gay fave, with a great bamboo garden in back. 344 W. 52nd St. (between Eighth and Ninth Aves., map D2), 212-315-2777, BAMBOO52NYC.COM **MODERATE**

HK Adjacent to the very popular slick man hangout HK Lounge, this HK serves up an eclectic and tasty Mediterranean/international mix in a stylish setting. Great for stomach-filling before heading next door or grabbing a bite before your bus back to Dubuque (Port Authority is just a few blocks away). 523 Ninth Ave. (at 39th St., map D1), 212-947-4208, HKHELLSKITCHEN.COM **MODERATE**

KYOTOFU You'll never again blanch at the concept of tofu cheesecake after giving it a try at Kyotofu, the Japanese dessert bar where you'll learn to look at soy in a sweet new light. 705 Ninth Ave., (between 48th and 49th Sts., map D3), 212-974-6012, KYOTOFUNYC.COM **MODERATE**

RESTAURANT ROW Although hopelessly tourist laden, this strip includes some decent options (the Italian-cuisined Becco at 355 W. 46th being among the most popular) that are undeniably convenient for a pre- or post-theater dinner. 46th St. between Eighth and Ninth Aves. (map D4), RESTAURANTROWNYC.COM

NIGHTLIFE

As the rising star—some would say already the queen—of mainstream New York gay nightlife, Hell's Kitchen is seriously cooking, with sleek bars like HK Lounge, Vlada, and the veteran but still strong Therapy generating the most heat.

BARRAGE Is it a divey lounge, or a loungey dive? The diverse mix of friendly locals who hang here don't care, especially during happy hour. 401 W. 47th St. (between Ninth and Tenth Aves., map N1), 212-586-9390

ESCUELITA Latinos and their lovers love this south Hell's Kitchen dance and show palace. 301 W. 39th St. (at Eighth Ave., map N2), 212-631-0588, ESCUELITA.COM

HK LOUNGE Sleek lounge pulling in an upscale party crowd. 405 W. 39th St. (at Ninth Ave., map N3), 212-947-4208, HKHELLS KITCHEN.COM

9TH AVENUE SALOON For a glimpse back in time to what pre-hype Hellsea gay life must've been like, check out the cheek here. 656 Ninth Ave. (between 45th and 46th Sts., map N4), 212-307-1503

POSH One never knows what one might find at casual and eclectic Posh, but it'll usually be fun and more often than not cute. 405 W.

MIDTOWN GAY TIMELINE

1903 The first recorded police raid on a gay bathhouse occurs at the Ariston (W. 55th St. at Broadway, map H1); 78 men are caught, 26 are arrested, 12 are brought to trial on sodomy charges, and 7 receive prison sentences of between 4 and 20 years.

1910 The tony Astor Hotel bar (1515 Broadway, between 44th and 45th Sts., map H2) becomes well known as a civilized meeting place by gay men city- and country-wide.

1930 42nd Street between Seventh and Eighth Avenues (map H3) becomes a rough and tumble gay strip, with sailors and hustlers cruising mid-block haunts like the Barrel House and the Marine Bar.

1940 One of many gays bars closed by the State Liquor Authority on grounds that homosexual patrons are by nature "disorderly," Gloria's (Third Ave. at 40th St., map H4) takes the SLA to court, and loses.

1950 In a nod to the hugely popular Charlie Parker co-owned jazz club Birdland (1678 Broadway, between 52nd and 53rd Sts.) that opened in 1949, a flock of gay bars with fowl names like the Golden Pheasant and the Blue Parrot create the Bird Circuit (map H5) of

MIDTOWN GAY TIMELINE

gentlemen's gay bars, fanning its feathers out from Third Avenue from the upper '40s through the lower '50s.

1955 The Mattachine Society of New York is founded and holds its first meeting at the Hotel Diplomat (108 43rd St. at Sixth Ave., map H6).

1958 Barbara Gittings holds the first meeting of the New York Daughters of Bilitis chapter, the first lesbian organization on the East Coast (headquartered at 27 W. 38th St., between Fifth and Sixth Aves., map H7).

1960 Front page *New York Times* article "Life on 42d St.: A Study in Decay" laments the prevalence of homosexuals on 42nd Street near Eighth Avenue, including details of the reporter's encounter with "a white youth with thick blond hair and handsome features who wore makeup on his eyebrows" who "spoke effeminately and shifted his hips and legs as he spoke."

1965 An association of local property owners and businessmen calls for what the *New York Times* pegs "a crackdown on Midtown's Social Misfits" in the area around Eighth Avenue and 42nd Street, including its hosts of "mincing perverts."

MIDTOWN GAY TIMELINE

1968 Representatives from seminal East Coast gay organizations including the Mattachine Society, the Daughters of Bilitis, and the Student Homophile League meet for a conference, part of which was held at the private gay Corduroy Club (240 38th St., between Seventh and Eighth Aves., map H8).

1975 Gloria Gaynor is crowned the Queen of Disco at gay club Le Jardin (110 W. 43rd St. at Sixth Ave., map H9) in the basement of the Diplomat Hotel.

1977 The legendary heavily gay Studio 54 (254 W. 54th St., between Seventh and Eighth Aves., map H10) opens, as does many a celebrity coke vial inside.

1981 *Love, Sidney* introduces America to its first gay lead television character, Sidney Shore (played by Tony Randall), who shares his Midtown apartment (136 E. 46th St. at Lexington Ave., map H11) with a single mom and her daughter.

1982 Thirty or so of New York City's finest raid the black gay Blues Bar (264 43rd St., between Seventh and Eighth Aves., map h12), destroying the place and severely injuring many, reportedly claiming their bullets were just "faggot suppositories"; no arrests are ever made, nor is an investigation even opened.

MIDTOWN GAY TIMELINE

1990 Greta Lovisa Gustaffson, the sometime lesbian actress better known to the world (from which she wanted to be left alone) as Greta Garbo, dies at her Midtown home (450 E. 52nd St., between First Ave. and FDR Dr., map H13).

1991 In support of the Irish Lesbian and Gay Organization who had been refused a place in the St. Patrick's Day Parade, Mayor David Dinkins gives up his front-of-the-parade spot to join the march with members of the ILGO (who marched without banners as part of another group) near St. Patrick's Cathedral (460 Madison Ave., between 50th and 51st Sts.); beer cans and angry slurs are hurled at Dinkins from the sidelines.

1994 The city finally shuts down the Adonis Theatre (693 Eighth Ave., between 43rd and 44th Sts., map H14), the last of Times Square's gay porn theaters.

51st St. (between Ninth and Tenth Aves., map N5), 212-957-2222, POSHBARNYC.COM

THE RITZ Older gents sip cocktails up front while gays of all ilks dance in the often-packed back at this Restaurant Row tavern. 369 W. 46th St. (between Eighth and Ninth Aves., map N6), 212-333-2554

THERAPY Now a Hell's Kitchen mainstay, Therapy serves up two sleekly-styled levels and a deliciously comforting bar menu. 348 W 52nd St. (between Eighth and Ninth Aves., map N7), 212-397-1700, THERAPY-NYC.COM

VLADA Hip and cruisey, Vlada's two floors pull in many of Hellsea's most handsome 'mos. 331 W. 51 St. (between Eighth and Ninth Aves., map N8), 212-974-8030, VLADABAR.COM

MIDTOWN

With its array of dazzling skyscrapers famous and not, it's hard to miss Midtown—and few do, accounting for the city's worst traffic congestion, but giving the area the hustle and bustle that makes Manhattan Manhattan. This is New York City's true heart, home to dazzling Grand Central Station, blinding Times Square, the Theater District, the headquarters of countless corporations, the United Nations, and a shopper's paradise including (but certainly not limited to) Macy's and the Fifth Avenue and 57th Street strips.

ACTIVITIES

So many of New York's most popular tourist destinations are in Midtown that it's hard to wander far in the neighborhood without simply bumping into one of them. Crowds or not, these are arguably the most bump worthy.

BRYANT PARK Gays have long been drawn to Bryant Park, turning it into a meeting place "for young fairies" in the 1920s and '30s. Today both fairies and non love this patch of Midtown greenery facing the grand New York Public Library. With a thrill for every season, it hosts the very popular Bryant Park Summer Film Festival (see listing in Film), it's home to the city's Spring and Fall Fashion

Weeks, and in winter there's The Pond ice skating rink. Oh yeah, plus free WiFi year round. 40th to 42nd Sts., Fifth to Sixth Aves. (map A4), BRYANTPARK.ORG

EMPIRE STATE BUILDING The world's tallest building from its 1931 completion until 1970 (when the North Tower of the World Trade Center reached past it), the Empire State is again New York City's loftiest, at least for now. Its views are forever priceless, as are its *Sleepless in Seattle*-esque romantic rendezvous possibilities. Advance tickets recommended for 86th floor observatory, $17 ($45 for Express Pass to bypass lines), $15 additional for 102nd floor observatory (tix available only on premises), open 8 AM–2 AM (last elevators at 1:15). 350 Fifth Ave. (at 34th St., map A5), 212-736-3100, ESBNYC.COM

MUSEUM OF MODERN ART (MOMA) Often pegged as the most important modern art museum in the world, MoMA's history has certainly been closely tied to the development of the movement, and will clearly continue to be so after a bold $425 million renovation in 2004 gave it 50% more exhibition space. Van Gogh's *The Starry Night* is here, as are Warhol's *Campbell's Soup Cans*. You get the idea. $20, W–M 10:30–5:30 (F till 8). 11 W. 53rd St. (between Fifth and Sixth Aves., map A6), 212-708-9400, MOMA.ORG

ROCKEFELLER CENTER A complex of 19 buildings spreading from 47th to 51st Sts. between Fifth and Seventh Aves., Rockefeller Center's offerings most worth checking out (other than the ice rink at Fifth Ave. between 48th and 49th Sts, open October to April) are NBC Studios and the dazzling 70th floor view-spot Top of the Rock, both at the building known as 30 Rock. NBC Studios Tour: $18.50, M–Th 8:30–4:30, F–Sa 9:30–5:30, Su 9:30–4:30. NBC Experience Store, 30 Rockefeller Center, 49th St. (between Fifth and Sixth Aves., map A7), 212-664-7174, nbcuniversalstore.com; Top of the Rock: Advance tickets recommended, $17.50, open 8 A M–midnight. 30 Rockefeller Center, enter on 50th St. (between Fifth and Sixth Aves.), TOPOFTHEROCKNYC.COM

TIMES SQUARE New York City's most famous street juncture has in the short course of a decade and a half been transformed from gritty crime and porn center to dazzling homage to commercialism, its tourist-crammed and Jumbotron-peppered backdrop now serving as broadcast home to MTV's *TRL* and ABC's *Good Morning America*. 42nd to 47th Sts. (along Broadway and Seventh Aves., map A8)

SEE ALSO IN ART: Marian Goodman Gallery
SEE ALSO IN DANCE: City Center
SEE ALSO IN MUSIC: Carnegie Hall

LODGING

Owing to the convergence of so much local commerce, Midtown absolutely abounds with hotelry options. While most are of the rather nondescript chain ilk, several stand out from the pack.

HOTEL QT Inspired by youth hostels, hotelier André Balazs opened the QT in 2005, playfully nicknaming it "the subStandard," and offering a bit of boutique chic at (comparatively) bargain basement prices. The swimming pool bar is a big draw, and is reportedly (if not officially) often clothing optional. 125 W. 45th St. (between Sixth Ave. and Broadway, map L5), 212-354-2323, HOTELQT.COM
MODERATE

THE LONDON NYC Formerly the Rihga Royal, the totally revamped London NYC opened in late 2006 as a modern

Anglophile's wet dream. Featuring high-cool lobby art by London-based photographer Wolfgang Tillmans and boasting Brit celeb chef Gordon Ramsay's latest eatery (called, rather appropriately, Gordon Ramsay at The London), the 54-story London also offers (relatively) spacious rooms in a great midtown location. 151 W. 54th St. (between Sixth and Seventh Aves., map L4), 866-690-2029, THELONDONNYC.COM **EXPENSIVE**

THE POD In perfect lockstep with the iPodifaction of the known world, the former Pickwick Arms has been recently reborn as The Pod, where accommodations are simple but stylish and savvy. Rooms feature a hip bounty of things you'd never expect to find in this price class: LCD TVs, iPod docking stations, free WiFi access, and waterfall showerheads. 230 E. 51st St. (between Second and Third Aves., map L6), 800-742-5945, THEPODHOTEL.COM **INEXPENSIVE**

ICE SKATING AT ROCKEFELLER CENTER

IN THE STEPS OF CARL VAN VECHTEN

Though chances are you've never heard of him, longtime Midtown resident Carl Van Vechten was one of the early 20th century's most trailblazing American writers, culture mavens, and shameless homosexuals. Born in 1880 in Cedar Rapids, Iowa, the tall, blond, and Midwestern Van Vechten moved to New York in 1906 after a brief stint in Chicago, where he'd fallen in love with ragtime music and African American culture in general. In 1909 he became the first American critic of modern dance for the *New York Times*. In the 1920s he became one of the most visible nonblack figures in the Harlem Renaissance, helping to spread the word of its myriad praises to white culture at large via a series of often controversial essays and novels. He befriended many of that movement's most gifted artists,

ST. REGIS John Jacob Astor's vision when building the St. Regis in 1904 was to bring Old World elegance to the New World. More than a hundred years on, the St. Regis is still the grand dame of New York hotels, offering unparalleled luxury and refinement to those for whom money is no object. The ultraposh hotel has provided temporary accommodation for countless international dignitaries over the years, and has also served as a more permanent home for the likes of Marlene Dietrich and Salvador Dali. 2 E. 55th St. (at Fifth Ave., map L3), 212-753-4500 or 800-759-7550, STREGIS. COM **VERY EXPENSIVE**

IN THE STEPS OF CARL VAN VECHTEN

including Langston Hughes and Countee Cullen.

Meanwhile Van Vechten became easily the hippest gay in the New York City of his day, his home at **150 WEST 55TH STREET** (between Sixth and Seventh Aves., map P1) playing host to a steady stream of sensational soirees throughout the '20s and '30s, attended by the likes of George Gershwin, Bessie Smith, and Paul Robeson. Though he was married to Russian actress Fania Marinoff, Van Vechten did little to hide his real proclivities, famously giving a character in his second novel—the, ahem, Duke of Middlebottom—stationery inscribed with the telling phrase "A thing of beauty is a boy forever." Van Vechten also maintained a long friendship with Gertrude Stein, who named him the executor of her literary estate. Van Vechten died in his beloved New York City in 1964.

DINING

Midtown has scores of dining options, many of them of excellent. Be warned that dress at the higher-end options tends toward business attire, and some actually require jackets for men (which most will provide).

AQUAVIT Swedish chef Magnus Samuelsson presents the city's premier Scandinavian eatery, winner of numerous awards in recent years for its sublimely modern take on Nordic favorites like herring and beef Rydberg, all served in a setting that feels like it walked off the pages of *Wallpaper* magazine. The Sunday brunch is one of the city's best. For slightly cheaper prices and a less dressy environment, there's the more casual Aquavit Café onsite. 65 E. 55th St. (between Madison and Park Aves., map D5), 212-307-7311, AQUAVIT.ORG **EXPENSIVE**

LE BERNARDIN One of the city's top restaurants for 20+ years, Le Bernardin serves sumptuous seafood a la chef Eric Ripert, who carries on the Brittany-born traditions of the founding Le Coze brothers. It can be a bit business-y, but always exudes Manhattan upper-crustic chic. 155 W. 51st St. (between Sixth and Seventh Aves., map D6), 212-554-1515, LE-BERNARDIN.COM **EXPENSIVE**

CARNEGIE DELI A 70-year-old Midtown institution and probably America's most famous deli, Carnegie has been a favorite of many a New Yorker over the years. Churlish waiters serve massive sandwiches with a side of Big Apple attitude. One of the few "true New York experience" tips that lives up to its hype. 854 Seventh Ave. (at 55th St., map D7), 212-757-2245, CARNEGIEDELI.COM **MODERATE**

DISTRICT This is an idea that could've gone very wrong: Theater District dining with a theater theme. It's pulled off nicely here though, with a relaxed stylishness and solid new American menu. Touristy yes, but as part of an evening of total Broadway immersion via its pre-theater prix fixe, it's hard to match. 130 W. 46th St. (between Sixth and Seventh Aves., map D8), 212-485-2999, DISTRICTNYC. COM **MODERATE**

SHOPPING

Midtown has been one of the city's most popular shopping destination for decades, serving as home to the flagship stores of no less than Bloomingdale's, Tiffany & Co., Bergdorf Goodman, F.A.O. Schwarz, and Abercrombie & Fitch (with its four-floor shrine to homo-eroticism) all within just a few-block radius of 57th St. and Fifth Ave. A few others not to miss:

COLONY RECORDS Showtuners and related singalongers will adore Theater District mainstay Colony Records for its unique stock of hard-to-find Broadway, karaoke, and sheet music stuffs. 1619 Broadway (at 49th St., map S1), 212-265-2050, COLONYMUSIC.COM

EMPIRE STATE BUILDING IN MIDTOWN MANHATTAN

MACY'S Sure, there are Macy's everywhere these days, but not like this one, the original flagship that Guinness says is still the world's biggest, with over 2 million square feet of retail space over nine floors. Film lovers will also know it's the home of miracles and the one true Santa Claus. 151 W. 34th St. (between Sixth and Seventh Aves., map S2), 212-695-4400, MACYS.COM

MOMA DESIGN & BOOK STORE With MoMA's 2004 renovation came this expanded flagship store, an ultratasteful collection of art reproductions, design items, and over 2,000 books. Check out the MoMA Design Store across the street at 44 W. 53rd St. for larger design items like furniture and home accessories as well as jewelry and gifts. 11 W. 53rd St. (between Fifth and Sixth Aves., map S3), 212-708-9700, MOMASTORE.ORG

TAKASHIMAYA Step out of the Midtown bustle and into the Zen-cum-spend Japanese oasis of Takashimaya, with six floors of pretty stuff aimed at soothingly beautifying you and your home. 693 Fifth Ave. (at 54th St., map S4), 212-350-0100, TAKASHIMAYA-NY.COM

NIGHTLIFE

While Midtown's gay bar options are definitely more limited than areas south and west, a few options remain.

O.W. BAR Named for Oscar Wilde, O.W. gets a friendly youngish mix and has nightly drag shows. 221 E. 58th St. (between Second and Third Aves., map N9), 212-355-3395, OWBAR.COM

THE TOWNHOUSE An "elegant gentleman's lounge" for "upscale professionals." 236 E. 58th St. (between Second and Third Aves., map N10), 212-754-4649, TOWNHOUSENY.COM

UNCLE CHARLIE'S Uncle Charlie's isn't the way you may remember the old one in the Village, but its relaxed vibe is a draw for those seeking a nice piano bar. 139 E. 45th St. (Second Floor, between Lexington and Third Aves., map N11), 212-661-9097, UNCLECHARLIESNYC.COM

THE WEB The Web is Midtown's only dance club, and the only Asian one in New York City. 40 E. 58th St. (between Madison and Park Aves., map N12), 212-308-1546, THEWEBNEWYORK.COM

UPPER EAST SIDE, UPPER WEST SIDE, HARLEM, AND WASHINGTON HEIGHTS

UPPER EAST SIDE, UPPER WEST SIDE, HARLEM, AND WASHINGTON HEIGHTS

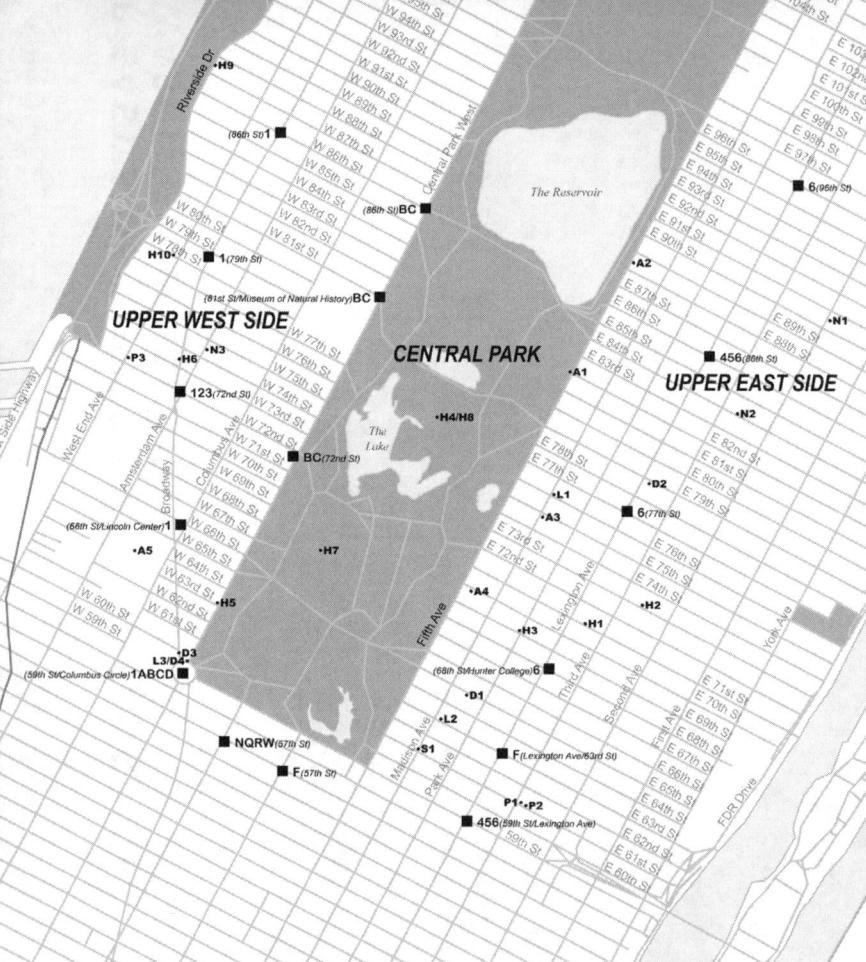

UPPER EAST SIDE

Long the home of some of New York's wealthiest, the Upper East Side was where the Vanderbilts and the Astors once lived and where the Soroses and the Bloombergs still do. The blue-blood invasion began in earnest after 1895, when Caroline Astor and brood set up camp at 65th Street and Fifth Avenue. As the 20th century dawned, the neighborhood's Central Park-hugging west side came to be seen by the city's elite as the only respectable place to reside in New York. Meanwhile to the East River-adjacent east, many immigrant communities settled, most notably the Germans of Yorkville.

Today, with Fifth Avenue's Museum Mile sporting many of the city's (and the world's) most important collections, and with those other gilded lanes Madison and Park just the next blocks over, the Upper East Side is still regarded as one of the city's most desirable neighborhoods—or stuffiest, depending on your point of view.

ACTIVITIES

METROPOLITAN MUSEUM OF ART A true New York treasure encompassing over 2 million square feet of gallery space, the Metropolitan Museum of Art (just "The Met" to locals) is one of the world's largest and finest art repositories, and recently opened its stunning new Greek and Roman galleries. From May to late fall (weather permitting), check out the Rooftop Garden Café, with fabulous park and city views. $20, open Tu–Th and Su 9:30–5:30, F–Sa 9:30–9. 1000 Fifth Ave. (at 82nd St., map A1), 212-535-7710, METMUSEUM.ORG

GUGGENHEIM MUSEUM Originally called the Museum of Non-Objective Painting when it opened in 1937, the Guggenheim moved to its stunning Frank Lloyd Wright–designed current structure in 1959, where it presents important art and architecture through innovative shows. From fall to spring, on the first Friday of every month it also turns the entire museum into a hipster club. $18 (includes audio tour), open Sa–W 10–5:45, F 10–7:45. 1071 Fifth Ave. (at 89th St., map A2), Upper East Side, 212-423-3500, GUGGENHEIM.ORG/NEW_YORK_INDEX.HTML

WHITNEY MUSEUM OF AMERICAN ART When Gertrude Vanderbilt Whitney tried to donate nearly 700 pieces of American art to the Metropolitan Museum in 1929, they turned her down, so in 1931 she created the Whitney. At its present location for over 40 years, the Whitney has strong collections of Hopper, Pollock, Warhol, and Haring among many others. It's also home to the Whitney Biennial. $15, open W–Th 11–6, F 1–9, Sa–Su 11–6. 945 Madison Ave. (at 75th St., map A3), 800-WHITNEY, WHITNEY.ORG

THE FRICK COLLECTION One of America's most esteemed small art museums, The Frick Collection, housed in the former mansion of steel tycoon Henry Clay Frick, boasts an incredible array of old masterworks including those by Vermeer, Rembrandt, and Goya.

UPPER EAST SIDE GAY TIMELINE

1961 Blithe socialite Holly Golightly (Audrey Hepburn) and thinly disguised gay neighbor Paul "Fred" Varjak (George Peppard) reside at 169 E. 71st St. (between Third and Lexington Aves., map H1) in the Truman Capote novella-based film *Breakfast at Tiffany's*.

1968 Mart Crowley's openly gay play *The Boys in the Band*—and the subsequent 1970 movie version—are set in an apartment on the Upper East Side.

1998 *Sex and the City* debuts, and main character Carrie Bradshaw resides at 245 E. 73rd St. (fictitious, but if it did exist would be between Second and Third Aves., map H2); her friend Charlotte York, after marrying Trey MacDougal, will move to 700 Park Ave. (at 69th St., map H3).

$15, open Tu–Sa 10–6, Su 11–5. 1 E. 70th St. (between Fifth and Madison Aves., map A4), 212-288-0700, FRICK.ORG

LODGING

THE CARLYLE Near Central Park and Madison Avenue's top shops, The Carlyle has been a rock solid luxury choice for over 75 years. International politicos and celebs (frequent stayers include TomKat and Britney Spears) are drawn by the Carlyle's swanky private home vibe, making it a preferred posh pied-à-terre. Downstairs, intimate song palace Café Carlyle is about as upscale old school gay as you

IN THE STEPS OF MONTGOMERY CLIFT

Most movie fans know that Montgomery Clift was one of Hollywood's most handsome mid-century stars, one who dabbled in same-sex affairs, and one who led a somewhat tragic life. What many don't know is the full scope of the tragedy.

Born in Omaha, Nebraska, in 1920, Clift showed acting prowess early on, and enjoyed a successful Broadway career from the mid '30s before starring in his first films in the late '40s. Slightly older than Marlon Brando and James Dean, he is often grouped with them as part of an intense breed of thespians to come out of New York's Actors Studio. Clift often felt overshadowed by the younger two, and that, coupled with his closeted homosexuality, led to an addiction to drugs and alcohol. In 1956, after leaving a party at Elizabeth Taylor's Hollywood Hills home, Clift drove his car into a telephone pole, and was famously saved from choking to death only by Taylor herself, who dislodged two of his

can get, with performers like Elaine Stritch and Eartha Kitt. But dress up, because CBGB this ain't. 35 E. 76th St. (at Madison Ave., map L1), 212-744-1600 or 800-227-5737, THECARLYLE.COM **VERY EXPENSIVE**

THE LOWELL Picked by the *New York Post* as the city's top hotel of 2007, The Lowell has just 68 rooms, allowing staff to dote more directly on guests. Just a block off Central Park, the hotel exudes old

IN THE STEPS OF MONTGOMERY CLIFT

teeth from his throat. Feeling himself horribly disfigured after the accident, Clift's addictions subsequently intensified. Marilyn Monroe, his costar in the notoriously surreal *The Misfits* (her last film), said Clift was "the only person I know who is in worse shape than I am."

Clift lived at **209 EAST 61ST STREET** (at Third Ave., map P1) from 1951 to 1960, when after a fire in that building he moved down the block to **217 EAST 61ST STREET** (between Second and Third Aves., map P2), a four-story townhouse that had once been a wedding gift from Teddy Roosevelt to his daughter Alice. Stories of Clift's wild behavior here abound, including his penchant for beckoning from an upstairs window for men on the street to come inside. Clift died here in 1966, a broken and no longer employable man. His reported last words, in answer to whether or not he'd like to come out of his bedroom and watch *The Misfits* on TV, were "Absolutely not!"

world charm in a very welcoming way. For a full NYC immersion, check into the Manhattan Suite, which features a multimedia homage to the city, and also just happens to have once been Madonna's pad. 28 E. 63rd St. (between Madison and Park Aves., map L2), 212-838-1400, LOWELLHOTEL.COM **VERY EXPENSIVE**

DINING

DANIEL For a sublime combo of true elegance and sheer taste bud delight, it's hard to beat Daniel, the eponymous creation of top chef Daniel Boulud, whose ingenious takes on fine French fare are served against a warm Venetian Renaissance backdrop. 60 E. 65th St. (between Madison and Park Aves., map D1), 212-288-0033, DANIELNYC.COM/DANIEL **EXPENSIVE**

CANDLE 79 Perfect for a gourmet vegan feast after a day at the Met and/or Whitney, Candle 79 is a bit pricier than other herbivore options, but well worth it with delectable dishes even meat lovers will savor. 154 E. 79th St. (between Lexington and 3rd Aves., map D2), 212-537-7179, CANDLECAFE.COM **MODERATE**

SHOPPING

Beyond Barneys, countless further genteel boutiques like Prada, Hermès, and Dolce & Gabanna run up Madison Avenue from the Upper East Side's southern 59th Street border to 72nd Street.

BARNEYS King of the New York style mountain, Barneys flagship store is where you'll find nine glorious floors of the latest looks at prices not meant for the faint of funds. 660 Madison Ave. (at 61st St., map S1), 212-826-8900, BARNEYS.COM

NIGHTLIFE

The gay pickings get slim this far north.

BRANDY'S Neighborhood piano bar. 235 E. 84th St., (between 2nd and 3rd Aves., map N1), 212-744-4949, BRANDYSNYC.COM

THE TOOL BOX Video bar and a basement of ill repute. 1742 Second Ave. (between 90th and 91st Sts., map N2), 866-674-9301, THETOOLBOXNYC.COM

UPPER WEST SIDE

Upper crust without being as, well, crusty as the Upper East Side, the Upper West Side actually got a much earlier start on its poshness, since its Bloomingdale Road (now Broadway) crossed through the heavily wooded neighborhood and became dotted with the country estates of moneyed New Yorkers even before the Revolution. Central Park's arrival was initially actually not a good thing for the Upper West, since it wrought an invasion by poor squatters from the south, anxious for a piece of parkside life.

Not until after the Dakota opened in 1884 as the area's first luxury apartment house did the neighborhood begin to take on its current air of finesse. Columbia University's move to Morningside Heights just to the north in 1897 was another milestone, giving the UWS a decided element of bohemia and intelligentsia not found on the UES's more staid streets. The early 20th century saw new immigrant communities arrive, including many Jews fleeing Hitler's Europe. In the 1960s came a large Puerto Rican, Cuban, and Dominican influx. And with its proximity to the Theater District to the south, the Upper West Side has long had a pronounced gay element, especially post–World War II.

ACTIVITIES

CENTRAL PARK It's nearly impossible to overstate the importance of Central Park to New York City. Historically speaking, its creation in 1853 (the first public park built in America) played a key role in the development of both the Upper East and West Sides in the decades that followed. Today as then, its 843 acres are a much-needed sprawling oasis of nature, recreation, and culture at the heart of the city, beloved by visitors and locals alike. Of course it's long been a gay-popular spot as well, especially the notorious woodsy Ramble section north of The Lake. Sheep Meadow (where the

UPPER WEST SIDE GAY TIMELINE

1947 Future gay political icon Harvey Milk, then a Long Island teenager, is reportedly arrested for indecent exposure in Central Park's Ramble (map H4).

1950 The Cork Club (south side of W. 72nd St.) is a small but popular gay hangout.

1960 The West Side YMCA (5 W. 63rd St at Central Park West, map H5) is reportedly a known male cruising spot, and as one patron put it, "virtually a gay hotel," despite management's best efforts to the contrary.

1967 Columbia University becomes one of the first colleges to recognize a gay student organization, the Student Homophile League.

1969 The infamous Continental Baths open in the basement of the Ansonia Hotel at 2109 Broadway, (between 73rd and 74th Sts., map H6); wildly popular on the gay scene, the Baths were not only a place to hook up, but to hear some of the era's top talent,

creatures for which it's named actually roamed until 1934) is also very gay popular, especially on summer days when its open lawn with stunning city backdrop makes for an unmatched sunbathing experience. The park is brimming with further options from boating to blading to biking, but another must-see spot is Bethesda

UPPER WEST SIDE GAY TIMELINE

including Peter Allen, Labelle, the Pointer Sisters, and Bette Midler, the last of whom launches her singing career here and earns the nickname "Bathhouse Betty."

1970 After walking from the Village in the first Christopher Street Gay Liberation Day March, activists hold the first "gay-in" at Central Park's Sheep Meadow (map H7).

1978 Sportscaster and Olympic gold medal figure skater Dick Button is one of six gay men severely beaten by youths with baseball bats in Central Park's Ramble (map H8).

1998 *Will & Grace* debuts, and the TV duo (and eventually Jack) reside at 155 Riverside Dr. (between 87th and 88th Sts., map H9). Their neighbors will include Nathan (Woody Harrelson) and Val (Molly Shannon).

1999 *Sex and the City*'s Miranda Hobbes buys her first apartment at 331 W. 78th St. (fictitious, but would be between West End Ave. and Riverside Dr., map H10).

Fountain, the first major public artwork by a woman ever to be commissioned by the city, and the site of *Angels in America*'s final scene. And though you wouldn't catch most locals dead in one, horse drawn park carriages are perfectly acceptable for tourists. They're catchable on Central Park South between Fifth and Sixth

IN THE STEPS OF LON OF NEW YORK

He may not be a household name even in gay households, but chances are you've seen Lon of New York's work at some point in your life. A major figure in the post–World War II boom in male physique photography, Lon's trailblazingly multicultural images graced the covers of many a magazine like *Superman* and *Strength and Health,* and became great favorites among gay collectors of the day.

Born Alonzo Hanagan in Massachusetts in 1911, Lon came to New York City in 1936, where he soon befriended gay neighbor and painter George Quaintance. Lon would later claim that in preparation for his first photo catalog in 1941, Quaintance painted "luminous leaves" directly onto the prints to remove hints of any naughty bits. Such humility and his steadfast refusal to shoot porn images unfortunately didn't save Lon from police raids, most tragically in 1961 when cops came to his Upper West Side home at **266 WEST END AVENUE** (between 72nd and 73rd Sts., map P3, and the former

Avenues and run about $35. 59th St. to 110th St., Fifth Avenue to Central Park West, CENTRALPARKNYC.ORG

LINCOLN CENTER FOR THE PERFORMING ARTS Once a seedy northern stretch of Hell's Kitchen, in the early '60s this several block expanse was transformed into the multibuilding minicity that is now New York's highbrowest hub of fine arts, including the New York State Theater (home of the New York City Ballet and Opera), the Metropolitan Opera House, Avery Fisher Hall (home

IN THE STEPS OF LON OF NEW YORK

home of no less than Mae West, the ornate detailings of which sometimes appeared as backdrops to Lon's work) and brutally beat him and destroyed and/or confiscated every single piece of his work. All that survived were those pieces that he had locked in a trunk. Devastated by the incident, Lon gave up photography for years.

Lon's excellence was rediscovered in the '80s and '90s by a new generation of gays, who appreciated his clear eye for Greco-Roman statuelike perfection. "I'd say, 'Now Sal, or Raul, or whoever, you're up there for one reason,'" Lon explained as a key to his work's quality in a 1999 *Village Voice* article. "You're there because you're an object of beauty. And you're supposed to think, I must be beautiful or I wouldn't be standing here. Keep that in mind and it'll come through in the pictures." Lon died at the ripe age of 87 in 1999, having finally had his first gallery show ever earlier that same year at Wessel + Connor (then on 26th St. in Chelsea, now in Brooklyn's DUMBO).

of the New York Philharmonic) and the Julliard School. Columbus to Amsterdam Aves., W. 62nd to 65th Sts. (map A5), 212-875-5000, LINCOLNCENTER.ORG

LODGING

TRUMP INTERNATIONAL HOTEL AND TOWERS Whatever you think of Donald Trump after his ugly mud-flinging throw down with Rosie O'Donnell, you can't go much farther the other direction tastewise than this understatedly posh 52-story glass palace at the

UPPER EAST SIDE, UPPER WEST SIDE, HARLEM, AND WASHINGTON HEIGHTS meeting point of Midtown, Central Park, and the Upper West Side. Roundly praised by critics and travelers alike for its stylish décor, cool ambience, spectacular views, and excellent service, the Trump International is in the top echelon of the city's finest hotels. One Central Park West (at Columbus Circle, map L3), 212-299-1000, TRUMPINTL.COM **VERY EXPENSIVE**

DINING

PER SE Napa Valley super chef Thomas Keller (The French Laundry, Bouchon) brings his elegant California flair to Per Se, an exquisite and intimate nine-course culinary extravaganza blending New American and French cuisines, with fabulous views of Central Park. Consistently picked across the board as one of the city's best. 10 Columbus Circle (at 60th St., map D3), 212-823-9335, FRENCHLAUNDRY.COM/PERSE/PERSE.HTM **EXPENSIVE**

JEAN GEORGES Another city-wide best list regular, this flagship of international star chef Jean-Georges Vongerichten is French at its finest, where you'll be nearly as dazzled by the presentation as with the unbelievable taste sensations from classic Gallic fare with sublimely unexpected twists (e.g., sea scallops with caramelized cauliflower and caper-raisin emulsion). Flawless. If price is a concern, try the same-kitchened onsite Nougatine, which is nearly just as lauded and even more inventive. One Central Park West (at Columbus Circle, map D4), 212-299-3900, JEAN-GEORGES.COM **EXPENSIVE**

NIGHTLIFE

CANDLE BAR Currently the only gay game on the Upper West Side, the tiny cruisey Candle Bar has been open since the mid '60s. 309 Amsterdam Ave. (between 74th and 75th Sts., map N3), 212-874-9155

HARLEM

Once a wealthy village where the Roosevelts and Alexander Hamilton farmed, Harlem's soil gave out in the middle of the 19th century leading to an exodus by the rich, a mass influx by Irish squatters, and a New York City annexation in 1873. A series of subsequent housing booms and crashes brought first European Jews, then just after the turn of the 20th century a wave of black settlers, thanks in great part to the work of black real estate entrepreneur Phillip A. Payton. For the first time in the city's history, blacks had a decent neighborhood to call their own.

As Harlem's fame spread outside the city, African descendants from the West Indies and American South flocked to Harlem in huge numbers, paving the way for the Renaissance of black culture in the 1920s and '30s that spawned wonderful and groundbreaking gay works by Langston Hughes, Bessie Smith, Ma Rainey, and Countee Cullen, among others. The Depression hit Harlem especially hard, leading to riots and unrest in the decades that followed. In the 1960s Harlem provided a major stage for the civil rights movement. Crime increased in the '70s, but by the late '90s another renaissance had begun, bringing new construction and a new excitement to the neighborhood that's even stronger today.

ACTIVITIES

APOLLO THEATER A world-famous venue and a neighborhood institution, the Apollo has launched the careers of countless black performers, and still hosts its energetic star-making-or-breaking Amateur Night every Wednesday. 253 W. 125th St. (between Adam Clayton Powell Jr. Blvd./Seventh Ave. and Frederick Douglass Blvd./Eighth Ave., map A1), 212-531-5300, APOLLOTHEATER.ORG

THE BLACK GAY AND LESBIAN ARCHIVE The culmination of years of work by Harlem writer Steven G. Fullwood, this invaluable collection of items from the gay slice of black history have since 2004 been part of the Schomburg Center for Research in Black Culture, which in turn is part of the New York Public Library and contains over 5 million historic objects. 515 Malcolm X Blvd./ Lenox Ave. (between 135th and 136th Sts., map A2), 212-491-2200, NYPL.ORG/RESEARCH/SC/SC.HTML

SEE ALSO IN MUSIC: Miller Theatre

LODGING

HARLEM FLOPHOUSE A living homage to the neighborhood's Renaissance period, Harlem Flophouse is a cool-oozing four-room brownstone and actual former flophouse, lovingly restored by proprietor (and artist/actor/playwright) René Calvo. Rooms are fairly big, funkily appointed, and named for local heros like Corky Hale and Chester Himes. 242 W. 123rd St. (between Adam Clayton Powell Jr. Blvd./Seventh Ave. and Frederick Douglass Blvd./Eighth Ave., map L1), 212-662-0678, HARLEMFLOPHOUSE.COM

HARLEM RENAISSANCE HOUSE Gay owned and operated, the Harlem Renaissance House offers "19th century gracious living in a modern world," its two beautifully restored rooms part of a lovely townhouse. Full bath, wireless Internet access, 24-hour concierge service, and use of the house's public rooms included, with further rooms rentable for events. 237 W. 139th St. (between Adam Clayton Powell Jr. Blvd./Seventh Ave. and Frederick Douglass Blvd./Eighth Ave., map L2), 212-226-1590, HARLEMRENAISSANCEHOUSE.COM
MODERATE

DINING

BILLIE'S BLACK This loungy gay-owned and run soul restaurant gets consistently high marks for its food, if not always for quick service. Especially great selection of Southern-style seafood. 271 W. 119th St. (between St. Nicholas Ave. and Frederick Douglass Blvd./Eighth Ave., map D1), 212-280-2248, BILLIESBLACK.COM **INEXPENSIVE**

MISS MAUDE'S SPOONBREAD TOO Skip the tourbused-in crowds at Sylvia's and head up to Miss Maude's, where cookbook author Norma Jean Darden serves up some of the neighborhood's (if not the city's) best soul food in a lively and friendly setting. 547 Malcolm X Blvd./Lenox Ave. (between 137th and 138th Sts., map D2), 212-690-3100, SPOONBREADINC.COM/MISS_MAUDES.HTM **INEXPENSIVE**

NIGHTLIFE

For the latest neighborhood goings-on check the Gay and Lesbian section of Harlem One Stop (HARLEMONESTOP.COM).

ESCANDALO NIGHTS (MONTHLY SATURDAYS) This very popular hot Latin boybash, long a monthly Saturday club at Washington Heights's Umbrella, moved in early 2008 to the second Sunday of every month at El Morocco Theater & Nightclub. 3534 Broadway (at 145th St., map N1), ESCANDALONIGHTS.COM or MYSPACE. COM/ESCANDALONIGHTS

SUITE While officially just barely south in Morningside Heights, Suite draws a strong Harlem crowd and is a fun attitude-free Uptown option. 992 Amsterdam Ave. (at 109th St., map N2), 212-222-4600, SUITENYC.COM

9

IN THE STEPS OF LANGSTON HUGHES

One of the most important figures of the Harlem Renaissance, writer Langston Hughes was born in 1902 in Missouri and grew up in the American Midwest before coming to New York to attend Columbia University in the early 1920s, a stay that proved short lived due to racial prejudice at the school. After taking 1923 to explore the world on a freighter, Hughes returned to Harlem in 1924. In 1926, his first book of poetry *The Weary Blues* appeared, immediately garnering him attention and praise.

After graduating from Philadelphia's Lincoln Unversity in 1929, Hughes traveled the country and the world again, reading his poetry to audiences, writing new works, and being inspired by what he saw from San Francisco to the Soviet Union to Spain. Throughout the period Harlem was his home base, and after World War II he returned here permanently, settling in the top floor of **20 EAST 127TH STREET** (between Madison and Fifth Aves., map P1).

A major voice of empowerment for black America, Hughes would never admit his homosexuality publicly, but often hinted at it subtly in his writing—or even strongly, as in 1951's *Café: 3 A.M.,* which chronicled a police raid on a gay bar. Since his death in 1967, Hughes's sexuality has been posthumously owned by the black community. In Spike Lee's 1996 film *Get on the Bus,* Isaiah Washington (in an ironic role given his later *Grey's Anatomy* "fag" fracas) beats up a homophobe, shouting, "This is for James Baldwin and Langston Hughes."

WASHINGTON HEIGHTS

Tragically undervisited by tourists and even by most NYC-living locals, Washington Heights is on Manhattan's far north side, unique in its hilliness, its array of Art Deco architecture, and its amazing Hudson River views. Getting its name from the fated Revolutionary War fort, Washington Heights has since the 1960s become home to the city's largest Dominican community, as evidenced by its nickname Quisqueya Heights (*Quisqueya* being Taino Indian for "mother of earth"). In recent years young bohemians and junior suits (including gays of both types) have started the march of gentrification, but the neighborhood thankfully retains its dynamic street-level zest.

ACTIVITY

THE CLOISTERS Overlooking the Hudson River on four gorgeous acres in Fort Tyron Park, The Cloisters is an arm of the Metropolitan Museum and home to a large chunk of its medieval European art and architecture collection. Incorporating authentic reconstructed pieces of five French cloisters from the period, this is one of the most beautiful and serene sites in all of New York City, and well worth the hike north. $20, open Tu–Su 9:30–4:45 Nov–Feb, till 5:15 Mar–Oct., Fort Tryon Park (map A3), 212-923-3700, METMUSEUM.ORG

NIGHTLIFE

NO PARKING Drawing a sexy and diverse crowd from the Heights and all points beyond, sleek lounge No Parking has established itself as Uptown's leading gay bar. Besides, it's hard to not love a place where karaoke night is hosted by Spicky Hilton. 4168 Broadway (at 177th St., map N3), 212-923-8700, NOPARKINGBAR.COM or MYSPACE.COM/NOPARKINGBAR

BROOKLYN, QUEENS, BRONX, AND STATEN ISLAND

BROOKLYN

East River

M7• •A1

(Bedford Ave) L ■   •N2
                         •S2

•S1

(Lorimer St/Metropolitan Ave) L   •N1   *Metropolitan Av*
                                           Devoe St

G *(Metropolitan Ave/Lorimer St)*

WILLIAMSBURG

•D1

■ JMZ *(Marcy Ave)*

BROOKLYN HEIGHTS

•H1
■ 23 *(Clark St)*

BROOKLYN QUEENS EXPRESSWAY

(Court St-Borough Hall) MR ■
(Borough Hall) 2345 ■   •P1   *Myrtle Ave*

                            MR ■ *(Lawrence St/MetroTech)*
(Jay St/Borough Hall) ACF ■

                            ■ 23 *(Hoyt St)*

FORT GREENE

C1/F2•   •C *(Lafayette Ave)*
         •G *(Fulton St)*

(Pacific St) DMNR ■ ■ 2345BQ *(Atlantic Ave)*

                                        Fulton St

                                        •N6
                          Atlantic Ave *(Franklin Ave)* CS ■
                                        (Nostrand Ave) AC ■

                                                    Bergen St
(Union St) MR ■   •N7
            •N3

•L1   •D2   ■ 23 *(Grand Army Plaza)*

      •N5   Eastern Pkwy
N4•   ■ 23 *(Eastern Pkwy/Brooklyn Museum)*
■ FMR *(4th Ave/9th St)*   •A2
                              ■ S *(Botanic Garden)*
PARK SLOPE   *(Nostrand Ave)* 3

      ■ F *(7th Ave)*

                    •A4
•A3

                    ■ L2

BROOKLYN

First-time visitors to New York City are often surprised to learn that showy Manhattan is not the biggest in her five-sister borough family; that distinction goes to Brooklyn, so populous with its 2.5 million residents that on its own it would be one of America's five biggest towns.

Brooklyn's importance to New York City's gay scene has never been higher, as more and more queer Manhattanites flee sky-high rents and over-gentrification for its more roomy, authentic,

OUT TRAVELER RATINGS GUIDE: BROOKLYN

GAY-FRIENDLY: ▼▼▼

GAY SCENE: ▼▼▼

LESBIAN SCENE: ▼▼▼

PRO-GAY LAWS: ▼▼▼

HIV RESOURCES: ▼▼▼

and at least slightly cheaper environs. While lesbian-heavy Park Slope and hipster-haven Williamsburg currently have the highest concentrations of homo settlement, others areas like arty DUMBO (Down Under the Manhattan Bridge Overpass), tony Brooklyn Heights, and rapidly gentrifying Fort Greene all have sizeable gay presences.

Meanwhile born and bred Brooklynites are increasingly raising their own gay voices, as in ethnically diverse Bushwick, which has been holding its own Pride march (in early June) since 2006. Borough-wide Brooklyn Pride, based in Prospect Park, comes every mid-June.

LODGING

Most visitors choose to stay closer to the center of action in Manhattan, but some have reasons for wanting to bed in Brooklyn, and local options are improving all the time. As a sheerly money-saving move for the short stay NYC tourist, it's unfortunately not worth the extra time (and cash) you'll spend schlepping back and forth to Manhattan.

HOTEL LE BLEU The first in a rumored coming wave of trendy hotels to hit Brooklyn, Hotel Le Bleu opened late in 2007 on the Park Slope/Carroll Gardens border, offering Manhattan boutique-style minimalism and a few things (like free parking and full NYC skyline views) that you'll never find on the island. Its 48 rooms aren't much bigger though, nor are the rates much smaller. 370 Fourth Ave. (between 3rd and 5th Sts., map L1), 718-625-1500, HOTELLEBLEU.COM **EXPENSIVE**

THE LORALEI B&B It may be far down most folks' lists of viable NYC lodging neighborhoods, but Flatbush gets a big lift from this charming Victorian home run by longtime owners Lance and Rob. Just two rooms here (one with an optional addition), but they're appointed with lovely period detail and come with great rates and incredible hospitality. 667 Argyle Rd. (between Foster Ave. and Glenwood Rd., map L2), 646-228-4656, LORALEINYC.COM

INEXPENSIVE

WILLIAMSBURG

Few places on earth have the dubious distinction of being so closely associated with the hipster phenomenon as Williamsburg, where thin is in and the ironic T-shirt is somewhat of a local costume. With its close proximity to Manhattan's East Village and Lower East Side (a quick ride on the L train, or the "Hipster Express" as locals often call it), Billyburg (another local term) by most accounts (especially its own) stole those neighborhoods' thunder in the early post-millennial years by becoming NYC's coolest place to live. Not surprisingly, a thriving indie music scene emerged, and this was the actual birthplace of the Electroclash sound thanks to longtime gay NYC club promoter and DJ Larry Tee. A recent flood of moneyed mainstream folk may have followed the hipster tide and pushed the ever-elusive true hipsters outward onto newer frontiers like Bushwick, but for now at least, Williamsburg remains Brooklyn's most tangible epicenter of cool.

ACTIVITY

GALAPAGOS ART SPACE Housed in a one-time mayonnaise factory, Galapagos now churns out a far less bland array of seasonings like amateur burlesque hosted by local queer fave Murray Hill, and Larry Tee's Saturday dance den Dizzy. (NOTE: Galapagos has announced it will be moving to DUMBO in the second half of 2008, where it will be NYC's first certified "green"

BROOKLYN GAY TIMELINE

1895 The career of Australian-born Lightweight World Boxing Champion Alfred Griffiths, known as the Young Griffo, comes to an abrupt end when he is accused, whether accurately or slanderously by a rival's camp, of sexually assaulting a boy at Coney Island.

1930 New York lies at the forefront of a national Pansy Craze, with overtly gay and drag performers like Brooklyn-born Jean Malin (and his song "I'd Rather Be Spanish (Than Mannish)") winning acclaim from mainstream audiences.

1940 The clientele at Brooklyn Heights's St. George Hotel (between Pineapple and Clark Sts. and Hicks and Henry Sts., map H1), at the time New York City's largest, is said to be heavily gay.

1951 Using the nom de plume Donald Webster Cory, Brooklynite Edward Sagarin's groundbreaking *The Homosexual in America* appears, becoming the first widely read nonfiction work written from a firsthand queer perspective.

1963 The State Liquor Authority revokes the license of gay hangout Heights Supper Club on Montague Street in Brooklyn Heights.

BROOKLYN GAY TIMELINE

1972 Greenwich Village gay boarding house resident John Wojtowicz takes hostages at a Chase Manhattan Bank branch (Ave. P at E. 3rd St., Flatbush, map H2) in an effort to fund the sex change operation of his lover, thereby providing the plotline for the film *Dog Day Afternoon;* the *New York Times* reports that the bizarre scene includes visits from Wojtowitz's gay friends, who "he kissed…in the bank doorway to the cheers of the huge crowd."

1997 The first Brooklyn Pride parade and festival is held in Prospect Park.

2006 GLOBE launches the first ever Bushwick Pride march.

cultural venue.) 70 North 6th St. (between Kent and Wythe Aves., map A1), 718-782-5188, GALAPAGOSARTSPACE.COM

SEE ALSO IN MUSIC: Music Hall of Williamsburg

DINING

DRESSLER From the man (Colin Devlin) behind longtime Billyburg faves DuMont and DuMont Burger comes this upscale and festive American-fared eatery, set within a beautifully appointed industrial interior. Great for dinner, or Sunday brunch mid-Bedford stroll. 149 Broadway (between Bedford and Driggs Aves., map D1), DRESSLERNYC.COM **MODERATE**

SHOPPING

Scores of trendy shops line the streets roughly spreading outward from Bedford Avenue and 7th Street.

A.P.C. SURPLUS This new outpost of the French clothier sells discounted past-season items, the brand's famous jeans, plus the latest in ironic hipster eccentricities like European military surplus stock. 33 Grand St. (at Kent Ave., map S1), 347-381-3193, APC.FR

OAK For the gracefully aging hipster in each of us, Oak carries such sought-after trendwear brands as Acne, Nudie, Opening Ceremony, and Y-3, as well as its own fab signature line. 208 N. 8th St. (between Driggs Ave. and Roebling St., map S2), 718-782-0521, OAKNYC.COM

NIGHTLIFE

METROPOLITAN Metropolitan is where it's at for the Billyburg gay, and for hipsters farther flung as well who hop the L for the cute crowd, cheap drinks, chill vibe, and (on summer Sundays) free back-patio burgers. 559 Lorimer St. (between Metropolitan Ave. and Devoe St., map N1), 718-599-4444, WWW.GAYBARSNYC.COM

SUGARLAND Super-hip and heavy on performance, Sugarland opened to a flurry of excitement in late 2007. 221 N. 9th St. (between Driggs Ave. and Roebling St., map N2), 718-599-4044, MYSPACE.COM/SUGARLANDBKLYN

PARK SLOPE

More conventional than Williamsburg and a bit farther away from Manhattan, Park Slope arguably has a stronger concentration of gay people, mostly lesbians who began settling here in earnest in the 1980s, giving it the not-so-flattering nickname "Dyke Slope." Increasingly their gay male brethren are also attracted to the neighborhood's beautiful streets and its family friendly smaller-city-within-a-city feel.

ACTIVITIES

BROOKLYN MUSEUM OF ART With a staggering million-and-a-half works spanning from ancient Egypt to contemporary America, the Brooklyn Museum is one of the country's largest art museums, and in New York City second only to the Met. $8, open W–F 10–5, Sa–Su 11–6. 200 Eastern Parkway (at Washington Ave., map A2), 718-638-5000, BROOKLYNMUSEUM.ORG

LESBIAN HERSTORY ARCHIVES This key repository of lesbian annals includes more than 20,000 books and 12,000+ photographs. Check the Web for opening times, which vary. 484 14th St. (between Eighth Ave. and Prospect Park West, map A3), 718-768-DYKE, LESBIANHERSTORYARCHIVES.ORG

PROSPECT PARK Locals cherish this large expanse of greenery, smaller than Central Park but much more tranquil, and home to the fantastic Prospect Park Audubon Center, Brooklyn's only zoo, and Long Meadow, a one-mile sweep of verdancy that's the longest stretch of unbroken meadow in any urban park. Map A4, PROSPECTPARK.ORG

DINING

STONE PARK CAFÉ With a great address on Park Slope's happening Fifth Avenue (and great windows through which to watch it all), Stone Park Café offers casual refinery, delicious food, beautiful fellow eaters, and a friendly staff: basically, exactly what you picture

IN THE STEPS OF WALT WHITMAN

New York's beloved de facto gay poet laureate, Walt (born Walter) Whitman was born in West Hills, Huntington, Long Island, in 1819. When he was still young his parents moved to Brooklyn, where they seem to have moved repeatedly due to bad investments, living on Front, Cranberry, and Johnson Streets in Brooklyn Heights. Young Walt became a writer and newspaper editor trainee early on, working in Brooklyn and Manhattan before returning to Long Island with his parents to start his own newspaper by age 20. For the next several years he would serve brief stints at newspapers all around the southeastern New York City area.

By 1850, responding to Ralph Waldo Emerson's call for a unique American poet to expound upon the country's virtues and vices, Whitman began writing what would become his life's work, *Leaves of Grass,* a deep and wonderful poetic indulgence of the senses (including to no small extent the sense of male love) during a time when such things were *verboten.* A good portion of *Leaves* was undoubtedly written at **106 MYRTLE AVENUE** (at Bridge St., map P1), his address in both the 1850 and 1859 Brooklyn city directories. Whitman printed the first edition himself in 1855, and almost immediately both praise (from no less than Emerson himself) and criticism (from those shocked by its immorality) came pouring in. Whitman would continue revising the book into several editions for the rest of his life.

Though *Leaves of Grass* brought Whitman some degree of fame, he did not see huge financial gain from it initially, and

IN THE STEPS OF WALT WHITMAN

he continued working as an editor by day. At night he would bathe and head to Pfaff's (Broadway near Bleecker Street) in Manhattan, where a bohemian salon held court. Whitman loved this, but he delighted just as much in the getting there via the Fulton Ferry (the inspiration for the later *Crossing Brooklyn Ferry*), where he could enjoy the interweaving of cultures—especially as it related to the working-class men who manned the boat. It's a theme that would recur with Whitman in the years to come: During the Civil War he visited wounded Union troops at the battle front, where he took a liking to at least a couple and wrote them long and rather melodramatic love letters to prove it.

Whitman was prolific throughout the 1860s and early '70s, and his career flourished. When he suffered a stroke and his mother died in quick succession in 1873, Whitman became depressed, and went to live in Camden, New Jersey, with his brother George. In 1884 he bought his own house nearby, where he lived out the rest of his years receiving visitors (like Oscar Wilde) and of course making tweaks to his masterwork. "Walt Whitman wishes respectfully to notify the public that the book *Leaves of Grass,* which he has been working on at great intervals and partially issued for the past thirty-five or forty years, is now completed, so to call it, and he would like this new 1892 edition to absolutely supersede all previous ones," said a *New York Herald* announcement in January 1892. "Faulty as it is, he decides it as by far his special and entire self-chosen poetic utterance." Two months later, Whitman died at age 82.

when you think of the perfect brunch. 324 Fifth Ave. (at 3rd St., map D2), 718-369-0082, STONEPARKCAFE.COM **MODERATE**

NIGHTLIFE

The ladies rule Park Slope's bar scene, but boys are welcome—or at least well tolerated.

CATTYSHACK Bileveled dancehall Cattyshack is always fun and draws a nice blend of varied lesbian types. 249 Fourth Ave. (at Carroll St., map N3), 718-230-5740, CATTYSHACKBKLYN.COM

EXCELSIOR Excelsior is also small and neighborhoody, but this one's more for the guys. 390 Fifth Ave. (at 6th St., map N4), 718-832-1599

GINGER'S PUB Ginger's Pub is a classic neighborhood bar, with pool table, jukebox, and booze. 363 Fifth Ave. (at 5th St., map N5), 718-788-0924

OTHER BROOKLYN NIGHTLIFE

Further afield from Williamsburg and Park Slope, gay (and gay-ish) spots dot the landscape.

OUTPOST LOUNGE Mixed artsy early evening café Outpost Lounge lies at the convergence of Clinton Hill, Prospect Heights, and Bed-Stuy. 1014 Fulton St. (between Grand and Classon Aves., Clinton Hill, map N6), 718-636-1260, OUTPOSTLOUNGE.COM

STARLITE LOUNGE Longtime black-owned gay bar. 1086 Bergen St. (at Nostrand Ave., Bedford-Stuyvesant, map N7), 718-771-3340, STARLITELOUNGE.PICZO.COM

BROOKLYN RESOURCES

BROOKLYN PRIDE 718-928-3320, BROOKLYNPRIDE.ORG

GLOBE (GAYS AND LESBIANS OF BUSHWICK EMPOWERED)
MAKETHEROAD.ORG/PROGRAMS/ORGANIZING/GLOBE

GRIOT CIRCLE Brooklyn's only elder LGBT organization, and the only one in New York City created by and for LGBT elders of color. 25 Flatbush Ave. (between Fulton and Livingston Sts., Fifth Floor), 718-246-2775, GRIOTCIRCLE.ORG

QUEENS

Talk about your big Queens: this cosmopolitan and easternmost borough is the largest of all areawise, and thanks to an unending stream of immigration will soon be #1 in population as well, say experts. Bearing a name that gays tend to find irresistible, Queens is home not only to a large Latino queer community centered around Jackson Heights, but also to growing presences in Astoria and Long Island City as well. Further pockets of pinkness are scattered all around this borough, which is so multicultural that the 7 train that runs through it is often called the "International Express" for its linking of Romanian, Colombian, Indian, Irish, Thai, Korean, Filipino, Turkish, and Afghan neighborhoods, just to name a few.

"In the last ten years, Queens has become the largest gay community in the area outside of Manhattan," Hector Canonge, who curates the monthly Cinemarosa film program (see Queens Museum of Art), told the *New York Blade* in 2005. "You don't have to go to Manhattan to see a rainbow of sexual identities and gender benders. You can see them right on the streets of Queens."

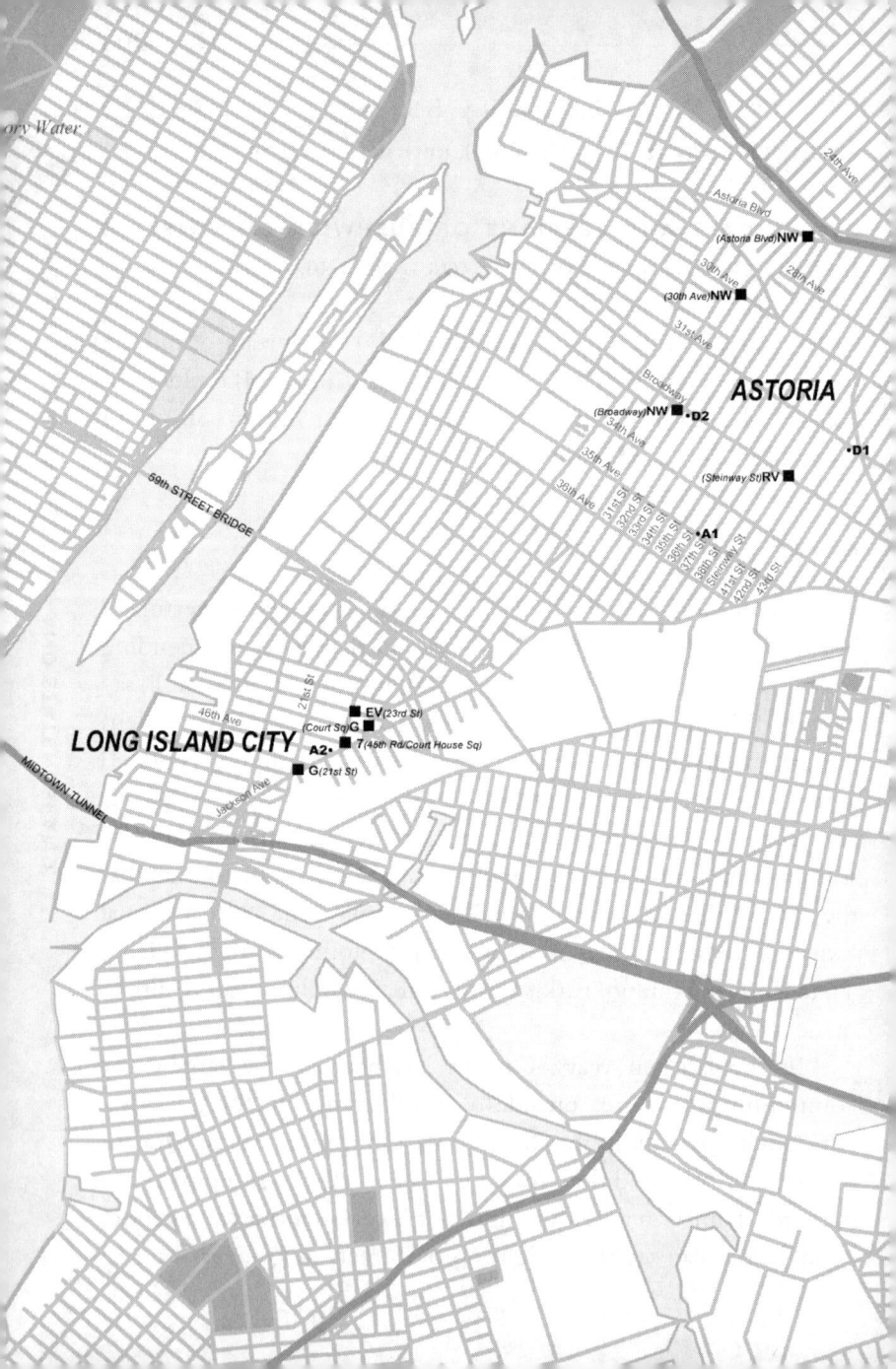

OUT TRAVELER RATINGS GUIDE: QUEENS

GAY-FRIENDLY: ▼▼
GAY SCENE: ▼▼
LESBIAN SCENE: ▼▼
PRO-GAY LAWS: ▼▼▼
HIV RESOURCES: ▼▼▼

ACTIVITIES

MUSEUM OF THE MOVING IMAGE Housing the nation's most important collection of motion picture and television artifacts, the Museum of the Moving Image's three floors of exhibits are complemented by a steady stream of theme-related screenings. $10, open W–Th 11–6, F 11–8, Sa–Su 11–6:30. 35th Ave. (at 36th St., Astoria, map A1), 718-784-0077, MOVINGIMAGE.US

P.S.1 CONTEMPORARY ART CENTER MoMA's most contemporary arm, P.S.1 focuses on showcasing emerging artists and is revered both locally and internationally as one of New York City's most cutting edge art institutions. Early every Saturday evening in summer (July to September) it also hosts the exceedingly hip P.S.1 Warm Up, bringing in DJs and music acts like Scissor Sisters and Fischerspooner. $5, open Th–M 12–6. 22-25 Jackson Ave. (at 46th Ave., Long Island City, map A2), 718-784-2084, PSI.ORG

QUEENS MUSEUM OF ART Housed in the New York City Building (originally built for the 1939 World's Fair), the Queens

Museum of Art is best known for its enthralling Panorama, a scale-model version of New York City originally built for the 1964 World's Fair and showing the city's nearly 900,000 structures. The Queens Museum also hosts Cinemarosa (CINEMAROSA.ORG), a monthly gay film series. $5, open W–F 10–5, Sa–Su 12–5. Meridian Road (Flushing Meadows Park, Flushing, map A3), 718-592-9700, QUEENSMUSEUM.ORG

ASTORIA

With its strong ethnic presences of Greeks, Arabs, and Brazilians, Astoria, with its close proximity to Manhattan, is also seeing ever-increasing settlement eastward from that isle. With a quickly coalescing gay populace, some locals are calling this a "Little Chelsea."

DINING

CAVO In a neighborhood with no shortage of great Greek restaurants, Cavo stands out for its smooth loungy vibe and its huge outdoor patio, and of course for its top-notch Hellenic fare. 42-18 31st Ave. (between 42nd and 43rd Sts., map D1), 718-721-1001, CAVOCAFELOUNGE.COM **MODERATE**

MUNDO CAFÉ & RESTAURANT For a friendly and more relaxed vibe, gay-run Mundo is an excellent choice. Co-owners Argentinean Guillermo Lucerofabbi ("Willie") and Turkish Canalp Caner ("John") inflect their native lands (and many others) into the great food, as well as their charming personalities into the warm place. 31-18E Broadway (enter on 32nd St., map D2), 718-777-2829, MUNDOASTORIA.COM **INEXPENSIVE**

NIGHTLIFE

ALBATROSS Neighborhoody Albatross is a friendly local hangout

QUEENS GAY TIMELINE

1967 Police raid El Baron Club (74-02 Eliot Ave., at 74th St., Middle Village), a private gay club where 200 people are present.

1969 As a mostly forgotten sidenote to history, NYC gay tempers were further flared just days after the Stonewall raid by news that a popular Queens cruising spot (southern tip of Flushing Meadows Park, at 78th Ave., Kew Gardens) had been virtually destroyed by tree-chopping neighborhood vigilantes.

1995 City officials order the closure of the Earle Theater (73-03 37th Rd., at 73rd St. and Broadway, Jackson Heights, map H1) after inspectors witness 40 illegal acts involving "at least 65 people," says the *New York*

with a diverse crowd, karaoke nights, and a daily happy hour. 36-19 24th Ave. (between 36th and 37th Sts., map N1), 718-204-9045, ALBATROSSBAR.COM

JACKSON HEIGHTS

The newest of all New York City neighborhoods included here, Jackson Heights was a planned district, developed less than a century ago as part of Edward Archibald MacDougall's vision for a community of European-style garden apartment complexes. Latin settlers from Central and South America (especially Colombia) make up a large chunk of today's Jackson Heights and are the

QUEENS GAY TIMELINE

Times; though it's allowed to reopen two months later with uniformed guards to "monitor sexuality activity," by the end of the year it's a Bollywood film palace.

2001 Queens gets its first and second gay centers when the Pride Community Center opens in Corona, followed by the Queens Pride House in Woodside.

2004 To protest LGBT exclusion from New York City's annual St. Patrick's Day Parade, Irish nationalist lawyer and activist Frank Durkan marches in the Queens Pride Parade instead.

2006 TV's *Ugly Betty* premieres, and Justin Suarez becomes Jackson Heights's most famous fictional gay youth.

backbone of its strong gay community, and South Asians are another very strong presence.

DINING

Jackson Heights is loaded with wonderful and authentic dining options. For some great cheap Latin eats, check out the curbside vendors along Roosevelt Avenue's 70s- and 80s-numbered streets.

JACKSON DINER It's no longer a secret, but Jackson Diner still serves some of New York City's best Indian food, with quick service, few frills, and an especially popular lunch buffet. Warning:

The fantastic north-Indian fare can get quite spicy. 37-47 74th St. (between 37th Rd. and 37th Ave., map D3), 718-672-1232, JACKSONDINER.COM **INEXPENSIVE**

NIGHTLIFE

Jackson Heights's Latin-dominated gay nightlife scene is booming, with the most popular spots all lying within a few block radius of the intersection of Roosevelt Avenue and Broadway.

CHUECA Queens's only lounge for lesbianas. 69-04 Woodside Ave. (at 69th St., map N2), 718-424-1171, CHUECABAR.COM

CLUB ATLANTIS The reigning king of dancehalls for Queens queens. 76-19 Roosevelt Ave. (between 76th and 77th Sts., map N3), 718-457-3939

FRIEND'S TAVERN Local gay mainstay. 78-11 Roosevelt Ave. (at 78th St., map N4), 718-397-7256

LUCHO'S PLACE Popular Latin dance club. 38-19 69th St. (at 38th Ave., map N5), 718-424-9181, MYSPACE.COM/LUCHOS69

MUSIC BOX Friendly jukebox joint. 40-08 74th St. (at Broadway, map N6), 718-457-5306

QUEENS RESOURCES

OUT ASTORIA Social group for gay Astorians. OUTASTORIA.COM

QUEENS LESBIAN & GAY PRIDE COMMITTEE
QUEENSPRIDE.COM

QUEENS PRIDE HOUSE/DIVERSITY CENTER OF QUEENS
76-11 37th Ave. (at 76th St., Suite 206), 718-429-5309, QUEENS
PRIDEHOUSE.TRIPOD.COM

BRONX

One Jonas Bronck, a 1630 Swedish settler to New Amsterdam by way of Holland, gives this borough its name, via his family's large farm (in what is now Morrisania) that was simply called "The Broncks." Mostly a pastoral backwater for its first two centuries, large numbers of Irish and then German immigrants settled in the Bronx in the 19th century, followed after the completion of subway and elevated train lines near the turn of the 20th century by several groups, especially Eastern European-born Jews fleeing cramped tenement-style housing in Manhattan for more spacious Bronx digs. By the mid-century came a Latin wave, especially from Puerto Rico and the Dominican Republic.

For whatever reason (many blame the massive neighborhood upheaval wrought by Robert Moses's major local freeway projects), the 1960s and '70s were a time of serious decline for the Bronx, as bleakly depicted in the 1981 Paul Newman/Pam Grier film

OUT TRAVELER RATINGS GUIDE: BRONX

GAY-FRIENDLY: ▼
GAY SCENE: ▼
LESBIAN SCENE: ▼
PRO-GAY LAWS: ▼▼▼
HIV RESOURCES: ▼▼▼

Fort Apache, the Bronx. Ironically (or not, since it's largely thanks to long overdue focused municipal investment) this area of the South Bronx is now experiencing the borough's most exciting revival, with artists moving into what's being called SoBro, including the neighborhoods of Port Morris and Hunts Point.

Still, gay life in much of the Bronx is undeniably tougher than almost anywhere else in the city. Deeply and often even dangerously homophobic attitudes are shockingly entrenched here in Manhattan's next-door neighbor. Fortunately there are signs of change, and some brave champions (particularly those behind the Strange Fruits media miniempire, the Bronx Academy of Art and Dance, and the Bronx Community Pride Center) are ensuring a brighter future for the queer Bronx youth of tomorrow.

ACTIVITIES

BAAD!/BRONX ACADEMY OF ARTS AND DANCE This 70-seat performance space and workshop in still-evolving Hunts Point is a trailblazer for the Bronx, nurturing a wide swath of local performance and visual artists who are women, people of color, and/or from the LGBT community. It also hosts the annual Out Like That! Festival (celebrating work by local LGBT artists) in June, and has become a de facto center for Bronx gay life. 841 Barretto St. (between Garrison and Lafayette Aves., 2nd Floor), 718-842-5223, BRONXACADEMYOFARTSANDDANCE.ORG

BRONX CULTURE TROLLEY This free(!) service offered by the Bronx Council on the Arts takes a trolley tour of some of the South Bronx's most exciting cultural attractions, dining establishments, and entertainment venues. First Wednesday of every month, except January and September, 5:30 PM. 718-931-9500 x33, BRONXARTS.ORG/CULTURE_TROLLEY.ASP

BRONX GAY TIMELINE

1997 Long-running Bronx-based high-camp gay soap opera *Strange Fruits (Fruta Extraña)* debuts on public access TV.

1998 The first-ever Bronx Pride parade marches down the Grand Concourse.

1999 Six members of the Lavender and Green Alliance, including New York City Councilwoman Christine Quinn, are arrested for attempting to march as openly gay people in the Bronx St. Patrick's Day Parade.

2006 A reorganized Pride committee holds the first Bronx Pride Picnic, the first Pride event in the borough since 2001.

BRONX ZOO The largest metropolitan zoo in the United States, the Bronx Zoo is home to more than 4,000 creatures and is one of the borough's most popular attractions. Favorite exhibits include the Congo Gorilla forest and the indoor Asian rain forest, which covers nearly an acre of the zoo's massive 265 total. Cost and hours vary by season. Bronx Park, Fordham Rd. at Bronx River Parkway, 718-367-1010, BRONXZOO.COM

DINING

BRUCKNER BAR & GRILL You can't get any more barely in the Bronx than Bruckner, lying as it does just over the Third Ave.

Bridge in the up-and-coming artists' enclave of Port Morris that some are calling SoBro. With its great (and cheap) comfort food, its smooth loungy décor, and its hip clientele, Bruckner is at the forefront—literally—of a changing 'hood. 1 Bruckner Blvd. (at Third Ave., Harlem map D4), 718-665-2001, BRUCKNERBAR.COM **INEXPENSIVE**

NIGHTLIFE

Bronx gay nightlife is hands down the most elusive to track of any area in New York City. A still very tangible antiqueer element in the borough forces many if not most gay Bronxers to have their fun elsewhere, which for the young tends these days to mean the Christopher Street Piers in Manhattan's West Village, and for older folks can mean just about anywhere but here.

CONCEITED (TUESDAYS ONLY) Secretive DL (Down Low) parties notwithstanding, the only above-ground Bronx gay option at press time is this Tuesday night party, which ironically and rather tellingly calls itself "Da Bronx best kept secret." Mi Gente Café, 1306 Unionport Rd. (at Westchester Ave.), 718-822-9274, MIGENTECAFE.COM

BRONX RESOURCES

BRONX COMMUNITY PRIDE CENTER Bronx's main gay social services hub. 448 East 149th St. (between Bergen and Brooks Aves.), 718-292-4368, BRONXPRIDE.ORG

GAY MEN OF THE BRONX Multicultural, multi-ethnic organization devoted to creating a safe and supportive environment for LGBT Bronxers. GMOB.ORG

HOMBRES LATINOS DE AMBIENTE (HOLA) Bronx-based Spanish-language organization for gay Latinos. 718-295-5690, HOMBRESLATINOS.NET

IN THE LIFE MINISTRIES An interfaith ministry dedicated to serving the LGBT community in the Bronx. ITLONLINE.ORG

STRANGE FRUIT RADIO STRANGEFRUITRADIO.COM

STRANGE FRUITS TV OR FRUTA EXTRAÑA TV (SPANISH) STRANGEFRUITS.TV or FRUTAEXTRANA.TV

STATEN ISLAND

Often called "the forgotten borough" by locals (in a recent *New York Times* article one resident used the more modern "goth borough of loneliness"), Staten Island is the least populated of the five boroughs and by far the most suburban in nature. The only borough not connected to Manhattan by a bridge, Staten Island is (though you wouldn't know it from looking at a subway map) actually much closer to New Jersey than it is to anywhere else in New York.

Post-native settlement began by the Dutch in the mid-1600s, but the island would be almost entirely rural for 250 years before the Staten Island Ferry first connected it to Manhattan's southern tip in 1905. Later in 1964 the Verrazano Narrows Bridge would connect it to Brooklyn, bringing an even bigger wave of settlement. Today nearly 40% of Staten Island's residents are of Italian descent, making it the heaviest Italian-concentrated county in the nation. Black, Latin, Russian, and Polish communities are also strong.

Though artists have begun sprinkling themselves across the

OUT TRAVELER RATINGS GUIDE: STATEN ISLAND

GAY-FRIENDLY: ▼▼
GAY SCENE: ▼
LESBIAN SCENE: ▼
PRO-GAY LAWS: ▼▼▼
HIV RESOURCES: ▼▼▼

island's north shore (especially in the neighborhoods of Stapleton, Tompkinsville, and St. George), Staten Island gay culture has unfortunately thus far been something of an oxymoron. Certainly gay people live here, but they're spread sporadically over the island. Gay-owned establishments have so far come and gone, unable to survive with the pull of more established Manhattan (not to mention Brooklyn and New Jersey), so strong for queer locals.

GETTING TO STATEN ISLAND

STATEN ISLAND FERRY Getting to Staten Island is one of the cheapest and more enjoyable transportation experiences to be had in all of New York City, via the Staten Island Ferry. The cost: free. The bonus: gorgeous views of downtown Manhattan, the Statue of Liberty, and Ellis Island. Except in the morning's wee hours, ferries run at least every half hour (every 15 minutes at peak times), and the trip takes just 25 minutes each way. Whitehall Terminal, 1 Whitehall St. (at South St.), Lower Manhattan to St. George Ferry Terminal, 1 Bay St. (at Richmond Terrace), Staten Island. NYC.GOV/HTML/DOT/HTML/FERRYBUS/STATFERY.SHTML

STATEN ISLAND GAY TIMELINE

1917 Brooklyn schoolteacher Gertrude Tate moves into Clear Comfort, the Staten Island home of her companion Alice Austen.

1987 Staten Island couple Sal Iacullo and Wayne Steinman become the first openly gay adoptive parents in New York State.

2005 The first Staten Island Gay Pride Parade is held.

2007 Staten Island native Anthony Wilkinson's *Boys Just Wanna Have Fun* opens at Actors Playhouse in the West Village, undoubtedly the first play ever to be set in a 1980s S.I. gay bar.

2007 Matthew Titone becomes Staten Island's first openly gay official when he is elected as the NY State Assembly representative from the north shore's 61st District.

BROOKLYN, QUEENS, BRONX, AND STATEN ISLAND

ACTIVITIES

ALICE AUSTEN HOUSE This gorgeous property at the entrance to New York harbor harkens back to a time when wealthy Manhattanites built their summer cottages along the Staten Island coast. Erected in 1690, Clear Comfort (as it is also known) was the longtime home of women-centric photographer Alice Austen, and it now serves as a museum of her life and times. $2, open

Th–Su 12–5, closed Jan. and Feb. 2 Hylan Blvd. (at Edgewater St.; take bus S51 from Staten Island Ferry terminal to Hylan Blvd, walk one block east to water and house), 718-816-4506, ALICEAUSTEN.ORG

HISTORIC RICHMOND TOWN With 25 acres of historic buildings (some three centuries old), Historic Richmond Town allows visitors to, in one place, capture unique glimpses of several periods of Staten Island and New York City history. $5, open W–Su 1–5, longer in summer. 441 Clarke Ave. (between Arthur Kill Rd. and St. Patricks Pl.; take bus S74 from Staten Island Ferry terminal to Richmond Rd. and St. Patrick's Pl.), 718-351-1611, HISTORICRICHMOND.ORG

JACQUES MARCHAIS MUSEUM OF TIBETAN ART Now over 60 years old, this wonderful and tranquil museum is the life's work of New York City-based collector of early Tibetan and Himalayan objects Jacques Marchais, and she herself designed the monastery-inspired building that now houses them. $5, W–Su 1–5. 338 Lighthouse Ave. (between St. George and Edinboro Rds.; take bus S74 from Staten Island Ferry to Lighthouse Ave., walk up hill to museum), 718-987-3500, TIBETANMUSEUM.ORG

SOUTH BEACH Miami it ain't, but to most but Staten Islanders this South Beach is an undiscovered gem, with relatively clean sands and waters and spectacular views, plus a long and nicely restored boardwalk with sporting and picnic areas. Father Capodanno Blvd. and Sand Lane, 718-816-6804

DINING

DENINO'S It's not fancy, it gets packed on weekends, and wee local children may be causing mayhem within, but it's all worth it for some of the best pizza in New York City. Gloriously cheap and delicious, family-run Denino's has been a cherished staple for Staten Islanders for 70 years. The sausage pie is a regular favorite. 524 Port Richmond Ave. (at Hooker Pl.), 718-442-9401

NIGHTLIFE

Totally gay-geared establishments in Staten Island have had a tough time staying open thus far, with Krave, Hush Saturdays, and Beanie's Coffee Shop all recently falling victim to the sparse climate. Two current good straight-but-gay-friendly options are within a block of each other in the Stapleton neighborhood: The Cup for coffee and Martini Red for, well, martinis.

THE CUP 388 Van Duzer St. (between Beach and Wright Sts.), 718-818-8100, MYSPACE.COM/THECUPOFSTATENISLANDOFFICIAL MYSPACEPAGE

MARTINI RED 372 Van Duzer St. (at Beach St.), 718-442-0660, MARTINI-RED.COM or MYSPACE.COM/MARTINIRED2006

STATEN ISLAND RESOURCES

COMMUNITY HEALTH ACTION OF STATEN ISLAND Providing educational and social programs for LGBT islanders. 56 Bay St. (between Stuyvesant Pl. and Slosson Tr.), 718-808-1300, SIHEALTHACTION.ORG

INDEX

ACKNOWLEDGMENTS

My deep and sincere thanks go to those whose previous hard work provided background information on much of the city's gay history and my understanding of it, most notably Charles Kaiser *(The Gay Metropolis)*, Daniel Hurewitz *(Stepping Out: Nine Walks Through New York City's Gay and Lesbian Past)*, Jonathan Ned Katz *(Love Stories: Sex Between Men Before Homosexuality)*, Luc Sante *(Low Life: Lures and Snares of Old New York)*, and last but certainly not least, the incredible George Chauncey *(Gay New York: Gender, Urban Culture, and the Making of the Gay Male World 1890–1940)*, all of whose great books I urge you to read if the small sampling of gay history in this guide piques your interest half as much as it did mine.